A Dictionary of Nigerian English Usage

A Dictionary of Nigerian English Usage

Herbert Igboanusi

Enicrownfit Publishers
2002

Published 2002 by
Enicrownfit Publishers
23, Ireakari Street
Mokola Roundabout
Ibadan

P.O. Box 14580
U.I. Post Office
Ibadan, Oyo State
Nigeria

ISBN 978-34225-5-3

iii

Dedication

For my father,
Mr. Emmanuel Igboanusi,
and my mother,
Mrs. Roseline Igboanusi.

Contents

Acknowledgements

My thanks go first to Professor Josef Schmied, who gave me the initial encouragement to write this book while I was on research fellowship to Chemnitz University of Technology. I wish to record my special gratitude to other members of staff of this University, particularly Dr. Andrew Wilson and Profesor Clarence Taylor, who shared their wealth of information on native English culture and usage; Barbara Krohne and Eva Hertel for several hours of invaluable discussion. I thank Alexander von Humbolt Foundation for varied research support, and Chemnitz University of Technology for allowing me access to their library and other facilities.

However, the dictionary project got a major boost with a three-month research visit to Humoldt University, Berlin, following a scholarship award by Fritz-Thyssen-Stiftung, Köln. I would like to thank the following members of Humboldt University for their invaluable comments and assistance during the preparation of this work—Professor Peter Lucko, PD Dr. Georg-Hans Wolf, Dr. Lothar Peter and Professor Klaus Hansen. Fritz-Thyssen-Stiftung deserves special thanks for funding my research stay in Berlin and also for sponsoring the publishing cost of this dictionary. I thank Dr. Frank Suder for his kind assistance. I also thank Humboldt University for allowing me access to their libraries and other facilities.

This work gained tremendously from the useful comments and suggestions of my thorough advisers. I am therefore indebted to Mr. Yemi Babajide, Dr. Francis Egbokhare, Dr. Mary Angela Uwalaka, Dr. Obododimma Oha, Dr. Isaac Ohia (all of University of

Ibadan), and Dr. A. H. Amfani of the University of Sokoto for their contributions.

I am particularly grateful to University of Ibadan for the time and facilities made available to me in the course of this work.

I highly appreciate the moral support of Professor Richard Taylor of Bayreuth University, Professor Jeff Siegel of University of New England, Professor Alan Brady of Kwansei Gakuin University, Dr. Yann Lebeau of Institute for French Research in Africa (IFRA), Dr. Mohammed Munkaila of University of Maidugri, Professor Kunle Adeniran, Professor Niyi Osundare, Professor Dan Izevbaye, Professor Ebo Ubahakwe, Dr. S. Oluwole Oyetade, Dr. Lekan Oyeleye, Dr. Philip Adedotun Ogundeji, and Dr. Duro Adeleke, all of University of Ibadan. Also appreciated is the kind assistance of Chief Kenneth Duru, Chief Isaac Onyeanusi, and Mr. Dennis Igboanusi.

This work is highly enriched by the works of prominent Nigerian English scholars such as David Jowitt, Adama Odumuh, Ayo Bamgbose, Ayo Banjo, Edmund Bamiro and Obafemi Kujore. It is also enriched by Michael J.C. Echeruo's Igbo English Dictionary. I thank them very dearly because their earlier works were widely consulted in the course of this research.

I also appreciate the contribution of Nigerian novelists whose literary works provided some of our examples. Special mention should be made of Chinua Achebe, Wole Soyinka, Elechi Amadi, Buchi Emecheta, Zaynab Alkali, Kole Omotoso, Chukwuemeka Ike, Timothy Aluko, Nkem Nwankwo, John Munonye and Cyprian Ekwensi. I sincerely thank editors of newspapers and magazines, and also columnists whose essays contributed the bulk of our examples.

Thanks are also due to all my undergraduate and post graduate students, who assisted me in carrying out a survey of market registers and fieldworks.

My deepest gratitude goes to my wife, Ijeoma, who despite the burden of family responsibilities, participated in the survey of market place registers and in secretarial duties.

While I thank all the persons listed here for their wonderful assistance, I have only myself to blame for any inadequacies.

Ibadan, March, 2002   Herbert Igboanusi

A Dictionary of Nigerian English Usage

1. Introduction

This usage dictionary attempts to illustrate the variety of English, which is peculiar to Nigerians—words borrowed from the many languages of Nigeria, English words, which have acquired new meanings in Nigeria, and words coined for local situations. A few words and phrases which are not Nigerian, but which have particular significance for Nigerians (e.g. step aside, austerity measure, ECOMOG, alhaji, etc.) have been included. The dictionary also includes colloquialisms, slang, and vulgarisms.

In a country where many languages are used, a great deal of borrowing among languages is likely to occur. Many borrowed words have been integrated into Nigerian English (NE). Their sources and their degree of popularity are also indicated. The inclusion of loanwords stems from the fact of their being used frequently in NE.

The entries in this work have been selected on the basis of their frequency in printed texts, and in speech (based on informants' and fieldworkers' judgements), and of their cultural and historical importance. We have, therefore, selected the most commonly used and the most widespread forms of expressions.

We have reflected the following linguistic categories in this dictionary: Lexis (loanwords, coinages, acronyms, intralingual compounding, semantic extension, semantic shift, translation equivalent, register, analogical derivation, ellipsis, collocational extension and reduplication); Grammar (functional conversion, "wrong" pluralization, prepositions, phrasal verbs, modal verbs), idiom, and style.

2. Nigerian English

In Nigeria, a second-language variety of English has been 'institutionalized' (Kachru, 1986: 19). As a former British colony, Nigeria has experienced a long interaction of English and indigenous languages, and this has led to the indigenization or nativization of English in the country. The nativization of English in Nigeria, notes Bamgbose (1995: 11), is not limited to the usual features of transfer of phonological, lexical, syntactic and semantic patterns of Nigerian languages into English, it also includes the creative development of English, including the evolution of distinctively Nigerian usages, attitudes and pragmatic use of the language. Therefore, nativization of English in Nigeria reflects the peculiarities of the Nigerian situation and its people.

Varieties of English in Nigeria depend essentially on the level of education (Brosnahan, 1958), exposure to forms of Standard English and the extent of mother tongue transfers (Banjo, 1993, 1995). This means that one may distinguish between various ethnic (mother tongue-influenced) Englishes, such as Hausa English, Igbo English, Yoruba English, etc, and also between the Standard NE and the various forms of substandard English (including Nigerian Pidgin), which is dependent on the level of education (Igboanusi 2000 & 2001a). Jowitt (1991: 47) aptly captures the picture of the varieties of Nigerian English in his observation that "the usage of every Nigerian user is a mixture of standard forms and Popular Nigerian English forms, which are in turn composed of errors and variants." These 'legitimate variants' (Bamgbose, 1998: 2) are contrasted with Standard British English forms.

3. Features of Standard Nigerian English

Nativization and the continuing influence of Americanisms are the most important characteristics of the Standard NE. Bamgbose, who identifies nativization as a notable aspect of Standard NE, categorizes such nativization into three aspects—linguistic, pragmatic, and creative.

Linguistic nativization includes substitution of Nigerian language vowels and consonants for English ones, replacement of stress by tone, meaning expansion, loanshift, coinages, integration of loanwords from Nigerian languages and Pidgin, translation equivalents, pluralization of some non-count nouns, conversion of grammatical functions, and some Nigerian language-syntactic structures. These features have been extensively discussed in Igboanusi (1998).

Pragmatic nativization suggests that the rules of language use typical of English in native situations have been modified to suit the Nigerian socio-cultural environment. Examples include: "sorry" (an expression of sympathy to one who has just had a misfortune, or to one who sneezes), "thanks for yesterday" (greeting for favour done the previous day), "well done" (greeting to someone at work).

Creative nativization manifests in the use of expressions, which are coined to reflect the Nigerian world-view. Examples include "area boys" (a group of social miscreants), "four-one-nine" (a dupe), "money-doubler" (one who dupes people of their money by promising them that he possesses the power to multiply their money), "second burial" (a more elaborate performance and celebration of the funeral rites for the dead).

NE has its origins in British English, and the lexicon of NE has therefore shown a strong British influence. More recently, however, there is an increasing influence from American English. Examples of American English vocabulary items frequently used in NE include "can" (tin), "eraser" (rubber), "movies" (pictures/cinema), "sweater" (jumper/jersey), "phone booth" (phone box), "shorts" (briefs), "custom-made" (made-to-measure), "kerosene" (paraffin), "toilet" (restroom), "generator" (dynamo), "duplex" (semi-detached), etc.

In Nigeria, English is today a commonly used language among individuals from a variety of linguistic and ethnic backgrounds. Among the educated, English functions as a lingua franca, and is the official language of government, business and commerce, education, the mass media, literature, and the law court. It is a compulsory subject in all schools (with the exception of a few Arabic schools), and is the preferred medium of instruction in most schools and tertiary institutions.

English therefore functions as a language of prestige and power.

4. The history of English in Nigeria

We will attempt to provide a brief history of the foundations of English in Nigeria as a way of tracing the institutionalization of English in this part of the world through the roles played by trade relations, missionary interests, and the colonial government. We observe that each of these eras laid the foundation for different varieties of English used in Nigeria.

4.1 Trade relations and missionary activities

The Portuguese were the first Europeans to visit the West African Coast. On arrival, they soon realized that communication was a serious problem. The Portuguese made various attempts to communicate with the natives, and the mixture of Portuguese variety of English and the various indigenous languages gave rise to what is today known as Pidgin. Some of the linguistic consequences of the early Portuguese contact include the introduction of such words as "palaver", "wrapper" and even "Lagos".

The influx of the English-speaking missionaries into the country started as from 1842. This, therefore, marked the emergence of non-standard or 'working English' (Omolewa, 1979: 14-15) which was widely used in Nigeria between 1842 and 1926. The 'Coast' English, which was already in existence following the arrival of

---

the Portuguese traders into some parts of southern Nigeria as from the 15th century spread to other parts of the country with the arrival of the missionaries.

By the middle of the 19th century, legitimate trade had developed considerably along the coast of what was later to become Nigeria, especially around Lagos in the west and in the Niger delta in the east (Osae, et al 1973: 105). With time, trade in slaves gave way to trade in palm oil, which now became the principal commodity. Increasing industrialisation in various parts of Europe led to an increasing demand for palm oil, which was available in several parts of Nigeria. The British merchants, whose interest became the concern of their home government, dominated the trade. Apart from its commitment towards the total elimination of slave trade, Britain also had missionary interest. During the course of the first half of the 19th century, British Christian missions had become active in various parts of southern Nigeria: in Lagos and Abeokuta in the west; in Bonny and Calabar in the Niger delta; and in Onitsha deep in Igboland.

The coming of the British and English-speaking missionaries in large numbers to the Southern part of Nigeria as from 1842 brought up the question of a language to be adopted for communication between the indigenous population and the visitors. Omolewa reports that English did not immediately replace the indigenous language for two reasons. Firstly, the missionaries had among them the Saro 'repatriates' from Sierra Leone who were versed in both English and the Nigerian indigenous languages and who could therefore serve as interpreters for their English-speaking colleagues and the indigenous population. Secondly, many of the missionaries began to learn the local languages in order to reach the people and spread Christianity. This was in compliance with the principal aspects of the missionary programme enumerated by Bowel in 1857 as quoted in Ajayi (1965):

> Our designs and hopes in regard to Africa are not simply to bring as many individuals as possible to the knowledge of Christ. We desire to establish the Gospel in the hearts and minds and social life of the people, so that truth and righteousness may remain and flourish among them, without the instrumentality of foreign missionaries. This cannot be done without civilization. To establish the Gospel among any people, they must have Bibles and therefore must have the art to make them or the money to buy them. They must read the Bible and this implies instructions.

These guiding principles of missionary activities in West Africa—the introduction of literacy, the training of missionary agents and the acquisition and interpretation of the Bible—meant essentially that the missionaries must have to develop and learn the indigenous languages of the people or train local people in English. In either way, the Bible must be read and understood by the people. So, many of the missionaries studied West African languages and also translated the Bible and the Prayer Book into those languages.

The missionaries were later to build up a pattern of

primary education at practically every missionary station. The schools had the common aim of propagating the ideals of Christianity and some of the basic doctrines of the particular denomination while teaching literacy and a little arithmetic.

The first question that arose was: What language were the children to be literate in? For most missionaries, the demand by the people themselves for English was decisive. Moreover, when the first mission schools were established at most of the large centres, majority of the missionaries had still to learn the local languages, which were being reduced to writing. Ajayi reveals that emigrant schoolmasters had themselves been brought up in English, which they saw as the language of commerce and civilization, and the road to success and advancement. The vernacular was seen as the language of religious instruction.

The early missionaries realized the importance of training their pupils through the medium of English, which soon became the major language of communication. They were assisted in this by parents, who "enthusiastically encouraged their children to learn and use English, the language of commerce, civilization and Christianity" (Ogu, 1992: 71).

When Hope Waddell arrived at Calabar in 1846, he found a flourishing busy trade in palmoil, which had brought the town as much prosperity as in the period of slave trade. English was the only European language spoken by Calabar traders, perhaps as a result of the predominance of English traders. While Portuguese was fairly widely spoken in Lagos, Warri and Benin, English was used in Brass, Bonny and Calabar. In fact, in Calabar, the 19th century missionaries found people who were keeping regular accounts and dairy in Pidgin English, and might have been doing so for at least, half a century.

Unlike the missionaries who worked hard to study and develop Nigerian languages, a new breed of Nigerians emerged who 'sought to establish close relations with the white man' (Omolewa, p. 17). These Nigerians who embraced the new religion attended missionary schools, obtained treatment in the newly established dispensaries and health centres and found employment with the European establishments. At whatever capacity they were employed—as cooks, gardeners, stewards, interpreters, clerks, guards, teachers, etc. —they must be able to communicate with their white employer. It is pertinent to note that these Africans were eager to learn English language primarily because it guaranteed a paid employment for them, which was far preferred to the less rewarding but more tasking farm-work.

It was not only the domestic staff of the Europeans that needed to speak English language. Many Nigerian chiefs and influential potentates also realized the need to be able to communicate with the white man who brought them expensive gifts, household items and luxury goods. Omolewa (p. 18) observes that with the coming of imperialism, the chiefs began to recognise the need for communicating with the European rulers in English.

4.2 The role of the colonial administration

The initial contact of Africans with different trading partners was 'restricted' (Schmied, 1991:8) and so, only rudimentary knowledge of languages was necessary to ensure communication. The developing lingua franca for these early contacts incorporated features of the languages used in the early Portuguese merchant ships and was enriched by African and other European languages. As has further been noted by Schmied, the variety of English spoken by the British sailors and their African crewmen in those days was characterised by many non-standard forms. On the other hand, the missionary era introduced the teaching of Standard English to West Africa. The colonial era saw many mother-tongue speakers of English migrating to these areas.

Trade relations and missionary activities could be said to have been the remote causes of the implantation of English in Nigeria by providing opportunities for early contact between the Europeans and the Africans. But the most important factor in the implantation of English in the country is colonization (Igboanusi, 2002). By the beginning of the 20th century, the colonial administration had been effectively established in many African states. The colonizers imposed their system of government on the indigenous people of Nigeria and expectedly, the language of the colonial administration. The acceptance of the British leadership also meant the acceptance of the English language.

Before 1882, the British government did not

participate directly in formal education. It was after this date that the government stepped in to establish guidelines for the organization of education and to emphasize the learning of English in schools. In 1897, for instance, one of the conditions the government laid down for giving grants to schools was the "effective learning and teaching of English language." In 1887, the education ordinance of 1882 promulgated in Gold Coast (now Ghana) was made to apply to Nigeria. Following this development, special grants were given for the teaching of English language.

'The colonial administration remained the single greatest carrier of English language and culture' (Odumuh, 1987: 10) and it was within this period that English became a second language in Nigeria. Odumuh observes further:

> The language of the Colonial Administration (the Civil Service) was English. Not only did the administrators help to 'spread' English language using bureaucratese and officialese: but more importantly in their homes they again did in their interaction with domestic staff—guards, gardeners, stewards, etc. In India these were the nurturing places, which manufactured Butler English; in Nigeria they were responsible for the rise of Nigerian Pidgin, non-standard Nigerian English, and NigE (p. 11).

The colonial rule witnessed the emergence of several newspapers and periodicals in English. The amalgamation of 1914 also facilitated the adoption of

English as a medium of communication in the vast colony.

It has to be noted that English language did not spread to northern Nigeria at the same pace with which it did in the south. The Muslim north resisted the western education and English, and instead preferred their Islamic education and the Arabic language. Western education (and by implication English) was introduced with caution, much later, to northern Nigeria. The acceptance of western education and English language in northern Nigeria was also with caution. This fact explains the uneven historical development of English language in Nigeria.

After the independence of India in 1947, the British began to realize that self-government would one day come to Africa. To further secure British political and economic influence, the colonial government started putting African colonies on the path towards modernization. In Nigeria, for instance, this modernizing programme brought developments, particularly in the areas of transportation, communication, 'extensive agricultural and industrial schemes and expansion of educational system' (Schmied, p.17). In the educational system, the new development policy saw the establishment of many secondary schools and a University College in Ibadan.

What is important in all this is that the British policy of modernization was implemented through the medium of English (Igboanusi 2001b). At this stage, English began to acquire enormous prestige as the language of modernization and the key to success.

5. Linguistic situation in Nigeria

Nigerian languáges are often grouped into "major languages" and "minority languages" based on demographic factors, status in education, regional spread, and availability of written materials. Major languages include Hausa, Igbo and Yoruba, while minority languages consist of all other languages spoken in the country. Bamgbose (1992) has, however, pointed out the inadequacy of the dichotomy (major-minority) as applied to languages since some minority languages are more equal than others. For example, Efik is taught as a subject up to School Certificate level, while Fulfulde also enjoys a special status as a language spoken in several countries outside Nigeria, just as Hausa and Yoruba. While the major languages—Hausa (in the North), Igbo (in the East) and Yoruba (in the West) are used as lingua francas for regional communication, the minority languages are used for "local (often) rural communication" (Schmied, 1991: 26) and are functionally marginalized to the "primary domains of life" (Webb, 1994: 181), such as family and friends, local markets and domestic services, traditional social institutions and religion.

Apart from the indigenous languages, which are the mother tongues of Nigerians, there also exist non-indigenous languages. They include English, which has become a second language; Nigerian Pidgin (the language in Nigeria with probably the largest number of speakers), which derives from the contact between English and the indigenous languages; Classical Arabic, which is learnt by Muslims; and other foreign languages such as French, German and Russian, which are taken as academic subjects at the secondary and tertiary levels of education.

The use of Pidgin in Nigeria is more popular in states that are ethnically heterogeneous (where it serves as the lingua franca) such as Edo, Delta, Rivers, Bayelsa, Cross Rivers and Akwa Ibom states. The heterogeneous states in Northern Nigeria use Hausa rather than Pidgin as a common language. Pidgin is also popular in Abuja and Lagos because of their status as Nigeria's federal capital territory and the economic capital, respectively.

Although English is spoken by not more than 20 per cent of Nigerians, the linguistic situation in Nigeria reveals the dominance of English in terms of spread, acceptance, and its official status (Igboanusi 1997: 23).

6. General aims

Nigerian English has special features. Its vocabulary contains a large number of words which are either not found in the Standard English or are used in ways peculiar to the Nigerian situation. As more and more Nigerians from different ethnic and linguistic backgrounds now write and speak English and English is taught in the early stages of education, it becomes necessary to reflect in a reasonably organized manner, as much as possible the richness and diversity of NE. This usage dictionary will enable Nigerians in particular, and the world, at large, to recognize the peculiarities of NE.

We have used a form of entry, which is different from that of known dictionaries, including the *Oxford English Dictionary* and *COBUILD*, because our meanings are completely dependent on the contexts of Nigerian usage. Therefore, we present a dictionary, which is a true reflection of daily use of English in Nigeria. However, McArthur's (2001: 15) observation—"Indeed, it is hard now and will be harder still in future for any dictionary or grammar of English anywhere in the world to be concerned with its home turf alone"—is still valid even in the present work. Our entry may also differ from dictionaries written in respect of South Africa, Jamaica and Caribbean because of different categories and contexts of English in use in these countries. The present compilation is primarily intended to be a dictionary of formal and informal usage.

Unlike a few dictionaries of similar traditions as NE, this does not cite references indicating where our examples appeared because our lexical items are words that are used in everyday speech and found in all Nigerian newspapers and magazines, novels, etc. All our usage and examples are from these sources as reflected in everyday use. We have avoided highly technical and specialized vocabulary, and have included only those, which are likely to be encountered very often.

We should also declare that this entry is only a usage dictionary and not a full dictionary. It is a collection of words, phrases and usage that are differently used from British English (BE). The vocabulary in it reflects the usage of Nigerians from differing educational and cultural backgrounds, different ethnic and linguistic groups and differing regional and professional backgrounds. Similarly, the items in this entry reflect the speech or writing of the educated (namely journalists, radio commentators, novelists, university teachers, students, politicians, and other highly qualified professionals) and semi educated (namely artisans, traders, carpenters, etc.). However, a word must be seen to be widely used in NE for it to be entered in this compilation. It is hoped that this entry is a representative collection of some of the features, forms, translations, adaptations, loanwords, and coinages characteristic of Nigerian English.

7. Research design

(a) Data collection

We have relied on our intuition as bilinguals in a variety of contexts. We have supplemented this with information from books, creative literature, newspapers and magazines, overheard conversations, tape-recorded spontaneous speech, and ephemeral sources such as letters, students' essays, invitation cards, handbills, and radio and television broadcasts. We have also used our students' projects on slang. We occasionally sought and received responses to a checklist of NE idioms and to an open-list of categories of Nigerian life—wedding, funeral, childbirth practices, superstitions, etc.

We also used our undergraduate and postgraduate students for data collection exercise in which we requested participants to compile technical items used in NE in their various regions. Items covered include Nigerian birds, indigenous fishes, animals, fruits, foods, forest flowers and plants, herbs, crops, timber trees, building styles, wears, folklore, folksongs, festivals, dances, music, religious expressions, indigenous games and sports, household idioms, etc. The authenticity of these data, as well as their nationwide popularity were established in a workshop with all the participating students. Some of these students also assisted in conducting a survey of market place register. In both cases, items, which are known only to particular markets or to a small group of people, were rejected.

(b) Methodology

We have placed emphasis on thoroughness of investigation and verifiability of information given in respect of every entry. This requires a concise description of items, using additional recognition criteria such as use, and contextual definition, where necessary. In all this, references are usually made to the British National Corpus and British English dictionaries, particularly *OXFORD* and *COBUILD* dictionaries. Items are entered on the basis of the frequency of their use in NE contexts. Where an expression is restricted to a particular social group, it is also indicated, e.g.:

Close   the less educated NE speakers use this verb in collocation with "light" where BE uses "switch off" or "turn off". Thus, "close the light" is equivalent to BE "switch off the light" or "turn off the light." In the same vein, "open the light" is equivalent to "switch on the light" or "turn on the light." In BE, the verb "close/ open" will collocate with door, booth, etc. but not with light.

In the case of loanwords, the source language is indicated, as in:

Ikebe often used colloquially to mean "buttocks", especially in descriptions of women, e.g. "She has a very big ikebe" (SL: Pidgin).

Jara the little extra quantity given free of charge to a customer over and above the quantity for which he has paid, as in "Madam, put jara." It may loosely be equivalent to "discount", although it is in form of additional quantity (SL: Hausa).

(c) Style and frequency

The degree of frequency of use of our entry is indicated by the use of such words as frequently, often, sometimes, commonly. The use of 'some', 'many' and 'most' to indicate the number of speakers that use a particular item helps us to know how widespread that word is. We have also specified the style of use—whether formal, informal, slang or colloquial. In some cases, we specify the register as well as the group among which a particular item is popularly used, i.e. students, Hausa, Igbo, Yoruba, etc. Where we indicate "also used", we mean in addition to the BE meanings of such words.

The label 'jocularly' is used where clarity is needed. Level of education of users is also indicated where a word is more commonly used by a particular group with such explanations as "more popularly used by less educated Nigerians" or "more commonly used at a lower educational level", etc.

(d) Spelling convention

We have spelt loanwords without tone marks so that such words do not sound "unEnglish". Accordingly, we provide phonetic transcriptions for such words so that they are not mispronounced.

(e) Patterns of Entry

1. The headword is always in bold type.
2. A phonetic transcription represented in double slash, follows the headword, usually only for loanwords.
3. Frequency of use is often indicated, where necessary.
4. Grammatical class is sometimes indicated especially in cases where there is a functional conversion of one grammatical class in NE different from BE, e.g. "mature"—while NE uses it as a verb in the past tense "matured", BE uses the ordinary adjective "mature", as in "Dan is not matured enough to drive a car." The grammatical class is also indicated where an item functions in more than one

word-class, e.g. "size"—it is often used as a verb in relation to wears to mean "fit", as in "This shirt does not size me. It is too small." The noun "size" substitutes for "cloth" in the NE expression "Cut one's coat according to size" which is equivalent to BE "Cut one's coat according to one's cloth."

5. More than one example may be cited if contexts of use are slightly different.

(f) Pronunciation Keys

Consonants

The consonants [p, b, t, d, k, g, f, v, s, z, h, m, n, l, r] have their widely accepted English value.

ŋ	as in Obong
dʒ	as in ojoro
tʃ	as in Och
ʃ	as in shekere
j	as in yam, wayo
ɲ	as in inyanga

The following double articulated sounds are lacking in English:

kw	as in tokunbo
kp	as in okporoko
gb	as in ogbeni
nw	as in nwaada
gw	as in ogbunigwe

Vowels

i	as in kombi
i	as in iba
e	as in gele
a	as in gala
a:	as in guard, saaki
ɔ	as in Ijaw
ɔ:	as in Ooni
ʊ	as in akanwu
u	as in kunu
u:	as in foo foo
e:	as in Jesu
o	as in obi, molue
ɔi	as in boy, moin moin
ai	as in kai, naira
ia	as in tufia
au	as in Hausa

Observations

In the process of verifying our information to determine their uniqueness to NE, we have observed that some of our items share common similarities with New Englishes, with African Englishes and with West African Englishes.

1.   New Englishes

In the case of New Englishes, similarities exist particularly in the pluralization of non-count nouns such as 'aircrafts', 'equipments', etc; the tautological use of some words such as 'assemble together', 'repeat again'; and in cases of the redundant use of some prepositions, as in 'discuss about', 'comprise of', etc.

2. African Englishes

For African Englishes, similarities are observed, particularly, in the use of the processes of omission and substitution to represent English idiomatic expressions. Examples include:

Omission "Blow one's trumpet"—"own" is omitted.
"Follow somebody's footsteps —"in" is omitted.
"Not by any stretch of imagination" —"the" is omitted.
Substitution "Add salt to injury" for BE "Add insult to injury"; "Develop cold feet" for BE "Get cold feet"; "As fast as lightening" for BE "As quick as lightening"; "Spread like bushfire" for BE "Spread like wildfire."

3. West African Englishes

As a result of Nigeria's population, its economic power, its military role in the sub-region, and its place as a centre of trade in the sub-region, it is common to hear NE coinages and even loanwords from Nigerian indigenous languages in other West African English-speaking countries, namely Ghana, Cameroon, Sierra Leone, Liberia and Gambia. Such NE loanwords (from indigenous NE languages and Pidgin) as "suya" (i.e. roasted meat with a lot of spices), "fufu" (pounded cassava meal), "egusi" (melon seeds used for cooking soup) are now known all over the sub region. Items known to be common to West African Englishes are marked in bracket as (Also in WAE).

Apart from this, some processes of lexical creation in NE also apply in creating other varieties of West African English with the result that the following similarities are shared commonly:

Semantic extension

The meanings of applicant, balance, brother, auntie, guy, and sorry have been used to accommodate the West African environment.

Reduplication

Words are reduplicated either for emphasis, pluralization, or to create new meanings, e.g. before-before (in the past), half-half (half each), now-now (immediately), etc. Reduplication in NE is generally influenced by the indigenous languages and Pidgin.

Intralingual compounding

Some words shared commonly through this process include gate fee (admission fee), go-slow (traffic jam), head-tie (scarf), motor-park (bus station).

Loanshift

This includes trouble-shooter as a troublemaker, son of the soil as a successful male indigene of a particular town.

It is as a result of these similarities that some scholars tend to suggest the compilation of a dictionary of West African English rather than Nigerian English. While we accept the existence of these similarities and the need for a lexicon of West Africanisms, we do not think that these similarities are enough to deny the peculiarity of NE. After all, there is a common Nigerian culture reflecting our foods, mode of dressing, building, music, indigenous fruits, idioms and a separate socio-political environment.

4. Nigerian English

Even in NE, there are items common to regions and ethnic Englishes. For instance, while the coinage "area boys" is used in the south to describe "a group of social miscreants," the loanword "yandaba" is frequently used in the north. Similarly, while the loanword "agbada" is widely used in the south to describe large flowing gown worn by men, "babariga" is used in the north for the same dress. Even within the south, while the loanword "abiku" frequently appears in creative literature written by Yoruba writers, Igbo writers use the loanword "ogbanje", both of which refer to "spirit children", i.e. "children that die and come back." What this means is that there is no one acknowledged variety of NE. What we have instead are varieties of NE. However, every word entered in this compilation is of special interest to Nigerians.

5.   Loanwords

In respect of loanwords, there are more widely used
Yoruba items in NE for obvious reasons. The first is
the role of the press, which is largely based in the Yoruba
areas. The second is the metropolitan position of most
Yoruba cities, particularly, Lagos (Nigeria's former
capital, and still the economic capital of Nigeria). Third
is the attitude of the Yorubas to always identify with
and project their rich cultural heritage. Other Nigerian
languages that supply the bulk of the loanwords are
Hausa, Igbo and Nigerian Pidgin. Demographic factor
and regional spread may be responsible for that. Sources
of loanwords are generally indicated after such entries.

Selected references

Ajayi, Ade J.F. 1965. *Christian Missions in Nigeria 1841–1891: The making of a New Elite*. London: Longman.

Bamgbose, Ayo. 1992. 'Speaking in Tongues: Implications of Multilingualism for Language Policy in Nigeria.' Nigerian National Merit Award Winners' Lecture, Kaduna.

——. 1995. 'English in the Nigerian Environment.' In Bamgbose, A., Banjo, A. and Thomas, A. (eds.) *New Englishes: A West African Perspective*, pp. 9–26. Ibadan: Mosuro Publishers.

——. 1998. 'Torn between the norms: innovations in World Englishes.' In *World Englishes*, Vol. 17, No. 1, pp.1 – 17.

Banjo, Ayo. 1995. 'On codifying Nigerian English: Research so far' In Ayo Bamgbose, Ayo Banjo, and Andrew Thomas, (eds.) *New Englishes: A West African Perspective*, pp. 203-231. Ibadan: Mosuro Publishers.

Brosnahan, L.F. 1958. 'English in Southern Nigeria.' *English Studies*, Vol. 39, No. 3.

Igboanusi, Herbert. 1997. 'Language and Nationalism: The future of English in Nigeria's Language Policies' *Context: Journal of Social and Cultural Studies* 1(1), 21–34.

——. 1998. 'Lexico-semantic Innovation Processes in Nigeria English' *Research in African Languages and Linguistics (RALL)*, Vol. 4 No. 2, 87–102.

----. 2000. 'Ethnic Englishes in Nigeria: The role of literature in the development of Igbo English' *Journal of Cultural Studies, Ethnicity and African Development*, 2.1, 219–230.

----. 2001a. 'Varieties of Nigerian English: Igbo English in Nigerian literature' *Multilingua: Journal of Cross-Cultural and Interlanguage Communication*, 20-4, 361–378.

----. 2001b. 'A socio-historical survey of English in Igboland' *CASTALIA: Ibadan Journal of Multi-cultural/Multidisciplinary Studies*, Vol. 7/I, pp. 48 – 59.

----. 2002. *Igbo English in the Nigerian Novel*. Ibadan: Enicrownfit Publishers.

Jowitt, David. 1991.*Nigerian English Usage: An Introduction*. Zaria: Longman Nigeria Plc.

Kachru, Braj B. 1986. *The Alchemy of English: The Spread, Functions, and Models of Non-native Englishes*. Oxford: Pergamon.

McArthur, Tom. 2001. 'World English and world Englishes: Trends, tensions, varieties, and standards.' *Language Teaching*. 34, 1 – 20.

Odumuh, Adama. 1987. *Nigerian English*. Zaria: Ahmadu Bello University Press Ltd.

Ogu, Julius N. 1992. *A Historical Survey of English and the Nigerian Situation*. Lagos: Kraft Books Limited.

Omolewa, Michael. 1979. 'The Emergence of Non-Standard English in Nigeria 1842 – 1926.' In Ebo Ubahakwe (ed.) *Varieties and Functions of the English Language in Nigeria*, pp. 14 – 26. Lagos: African Universities Press.

A

aa! /a:/ an interjection, which expresses strong surprise, amounting to disbelief, e.g.
A: The director is now going out with Bimpe.
B: Aa! I just hope her husband doesn't hear this.

Aare Ona Kakanfo /a:re ɔna kakanfɔ/ a chieftaincy title in Yorubaland, meaning "the Generalissimo of Yorubaland", as in "Aare Ona Kakanfo of Yorubaland." (SL: Yoruba).

a fast guy a fraudster; a trickster, as in "The boy is a fast guy" for BE "The boy is a fraudster."

a whole frequently used in NE to express surprise that one did something demeaning to one's status, e.g. "Why should you insult a whole king?" for BE "Why should you insult a person of the King's calibre?"

abacha /abatʃa/ sliced cassava flakes or tapioca flakes. "Abacha" may be prepared with oil and other ingredients as salad or may simply be eaten with coconut, groundnut, etc. (SL: Igbo).

abada /abada/ wax printed cloth; wax print; printed cloth; one or two-piece waist wraps tied over the waist by women and reaches the ankle, as in "Have you any left-over abada today?" (SL: Igbo).

---

abandoned projects contracts for which money was collected but work left undone, as in "During his campaign for election as governor of Anambra state, Chinwoke Mbadinuju promised to constitute a probe panel to review on-going and abandoned projects in the state."

abandoned property a phrase frequently used to refer to the property of Igbo people seized in some states, particularly Rivers State, after the civil war, as in "In spite of 'no victors no vanquished', the Igbos in Nigeria are still battling with abandoned properties with their immediate neighbours some 28 years after the civil war."

abi? /abi/ an interjection often used as a way of confirming information. It may be equivalent to "isn't it?", e.g.
A: Tomorrow is your birthday, abi?
B: Yes.
(SL: Yoruba)

abiku /abiku/ used as a loanword by the Yoruba to refer to a child that dies and comes back to life. "Abiku" is equivalent to "ogbanje" in Igbo. Like "ogbanje", "abiku children" have today come to be known as "spirit children". (SL: Yoruba).

aboki /aboki/ "friend", commonly used in the northern part of Nigeria. It can be used to address an unknown person as a polite way of attracting his attention, as in "Aboki, can you show me the way to the Emir's palace?" (SL: Hausa).

abreast the preposition "with" substitutes for "of" in the NE idiomatic expression "keep abreast with" which is equivalent to BE "keep abreast of", e.g. "You should always try to keep abreast with developments in the country" for "You should always try to keep abreast of developments in the country."

abstain in NE but not in BE, this verb is frequently found in the phrase "abstain from work/duty", as in "The Governor has asked Directors-General to compile the names of workers who often abstain from work." In BE, this verb is frequently used in the phrase "abstain from voting." Also, in a formal or jocular language, it may occur in BE with the meaning "to keep oneself from doing or having something that one likes or enjoys", as in "abstain from alcohol."

Abuja /abʊdʒa/ the federal capital territory of Nigeria.

Abuja yam /abʊdʒa jæm/ a variety of "white yam" said to be produced within Abuja environs, e.g. "We have Abuja yam."

abuse while BE employs this word in figurative expressions, with the meaning "to speak in an insulting or offensive way to or about something", as in "Journalists had been threatened and abused", it is used singularly in NE to mean "rebuke", "insult", as in "I abused them for coming late."

a/c an abbreviation for "air-conditioner" which is frequently found in NE, e.g. "Never sleep with your a/c on." Speakers of BE normally prefer the full form.

Aburi accord frequently used to refer to the agreement signed in Aburi (a city in Ghana) by both the Federal Government team led by Yakubu Gowon and the Biafran team led by Chukwuemeka Ojukwu, which supported confederation as a way of resolving the crisis in Nigeria in 1967. Gowon later rejected this accord, and this, among other factors, led to the Nigerian civil war.

acada /akada/ clipped form of "academician" or "academics" i.e. educated people, e.g. "These acada people are very intelligent" for BE "These educated people are very intelligent"; "How is acada?" for BE "How are your studies?"

acada woman /akada wʊmən/ refers to a female undergraduate or graduate who is seen to be educated and therefore 'wise'.

academic-people an intralingual collocation which is lacking in BE. It refers to the educated people, especially university lecturers, e.g. "These academic-people are always going on strike."

academicians often used to also mean "academics". It is used to refer to teachers, especially in higher educational institutions, e.g. "Academicians are poorly remunerated in Nigeria." In BE, it refers to a member of an academy.

academics often used to mean academic work or activities or even the profession itself, as in "Why I like academics is that it gives me enough time to do other things" for BE "Why I like academic job/teaching is that it gives me enough time to do other things." In BE, 'academics' refers to 'academic persons.'

act frequently used to mean 'incident' e.g. "all the people who were implicated in the act will be punished."

action it has an extended meaning "to find solution to a problem", e.g. "The minister of education has been directed to take action on that matter with immediate effect."

actually often used especially at the lower educational level as an exclamation to express agreement or support to a previous statement or question. It may also mean "yes" or "That's right", as in:
A: Marriage is expensive in Igboland.
B: Actually.

AD an abbreviation for Alliance for Democracy, one of Nigeria's political parties.

adequate enough in NE, it is common to find "enough" in collocation with "adequate", e.g. "The measures outlined in this year's budget are adequate enough to stimulate growth and reduce inflation, if they are well-implemented." In BE, "enough" would be tautological in this sentence since "adequate" is sufficient to express the meaning intended.

adire /adire/ used as a loanword to mean a colourfully designed and painted wear worn by both men and women. (SL: Yoruba).

---

adulterated kerosene killer kerosene, which is suspected to be mixed with petrol, and which often explodes while in use, inflicting injuries on its victims, ranging from burns to death, e.g. "Adulterated kerosene has so far killed ten persons in Lagos State."

advice often used with an indefinite article when it means "counsel", e.g. "I gave him a good advice as a friend." "Advices" is sometimes used for BE "pieces of advice". This noun is treated in BE as non-count and is consequently not preceded by the indefinite article.

advocate for the particle "for" frequently follows the verb "advocate" in NE in contexts where it will not occur in BE, e.g. "The military governor stated that those advocating for the break-up of the country are doing that for their selfish interests." In BE usage, this particle will be considered redundant in the above sentence.

afa /afa/ divination; consultation with deities regarding past or future events by 'throwing' and 'reading' cowries, animal teeth, coins, etc; an oracle, as in "A prominent afa man was consulted before the community took the decision to ostracise the man." (SL: Igbo).

afang /afaŋ/ used as a loanword for popular vegetable soup among the Efik, as in "Afang soup". (SL: Efik).

AFEM an acronym for Autonomous Foreign Exchange Market.

Afenifere /afenifere/ used as a loanword meaning "we wish others well", it is a socio-political organization of

Yoruba people, as in "A pan-Yoruba organization, Afenifere group will meet Thursday in Ijebu Igbo for what a member described as 'crucial to the interest of our people'." (SL: Yoruba).

affair ellipsis for "sexual affair". "Affair" is commonly used in NE to mean "sex", as in "His wife confirmed that the landlord once had an affair with her in her husband's bedroom." A BE speaker would prefer to use "sex" or "sexual affair" rather than "affair" in the above sentence.

afo /afɔ/ third day of the four-day Igbo week; market that holds on Afo day, as in "Afo is a big day in our community because it is a day that everyone comes to the market either to buy or to sell goods." Other market days are "nkwo", "eke" and "oye". (SL: Igbo).

AFRC an abbreviation for Armed Forces Ruling Council, the highest decision making body of the federal military government or "the military parliament."

African time colloquially used as a jocular reference to unpunctuality, e.g. "The meeting will start at exactly 3 p.m. Please be punctual. No African time."

afro-beat /afrobiːt/ a coinage for a brand of African music popularized by a well-known controversial Nigerian musician, Fela Anikulapo Kuti. "Afro-beat music" is a commonly heard NE collocation that refers to this brand of music.

after as an adverb, it is used to mean "later", "later on", "afterwards", e.g. "I will tell you after" for "I will

---

tell you later on."

As a preposition, it is used to express time, e.g.:

A: What is the time?

B: Ten after one (for BE "Ten past one").

Another commonly heard NE expression involves the use of "after" + a period of time, e.g. "Call back after thirty minutes" for BE "Call back in thirty minutes time."

afterall formed in agglutination for BE 'after all'.

again an adverbial particle frequently used to mean "indeed", "else", "anymore", "any longer", e.g. "Who again will pay my fees now that my sponsor is dead?" "Who again...?" in this context is equivalent to BE "Who else...?"; "I have nothing again" for BE "I have nothing left"; "He doesn't live here again" for BE "He doesn't live here any more"; "They have been waiting for a long time, and cannot wait again" for BE "They have been waiting for a long time and cannot wait any longer." Also, many NE speakers often say: "Repeat again." In BE, "again" here will be unnecessary.

agbada /agbada/ a large flowing gown worn by men, often embroidered at the neck and cuffs. A complete agbada consists of a gown, a shirt and a pair of trousers made up of the same materials, e.g. "He said good-bye and swept out of the room in his agbada made from an expensive lace material." (SL: Yoruba).

Agbekoya /agbekɔja/ a farmers' resistance movement, which fought for improved standard of living and equitable prices for their products, between 1968 and

1969, in the Southwest. They were later used during the 1979 and 1983 elections as a kind of stand-by army for the Southwest. (SL: Yoruba).

agbero/agboro /agbero/ a motor park tout, as in "Yesterday, police in Lagos jailed 150 touts or agberos as they are popularly called in Lagos." "Agboro" is the Igbo equivalent of Yoruba`s "agbero". (SL: Yoruba).

agbo /agbo/ local medicine in liquid form. (SL: Yoruba).

age-grade used to describe a group of people belonging to the same age group forming a socio-cultural group whose duty is to contribute to the development of their community, as in "Chukwu's wedding was boycotted by the members of his age-grade because he did not invite them officially."

age-mate used to describe somebody in the same age group with another person, as in "Obi and Uche are the same age-mate."

agidi /agidi/ cream of corn; blancmange made from guinea corn; meal prepared from ground maize and often wrapped in pieces of plantain or other leaves, as in "She did not want anything, not any more, not from these people who had tricked her into letting Okoli out of her sight because of some hot agidi." It is known as "eko" in Yoruba. (SL: Igbo).

Ahiajoku /ahiadʒɔkʊ/ Yam god; New Yam Festival; an annual harvest festival marking the formal harvest of new yam, and paying tribute to the yam god, e.g. "This year's Ahiajoku lecture has been fixed for the last Friday of November, 2001." (SL: Igbo).

aid this noun is often found in the plural form in NE, as in "The country has lost several billions of dollars in investment and foreign aids since the annulment of June 12 election believed to have been won by Chief Abiola." When this noun refers to financial assistance, it is normally non-count and so not pluralized with -s in BE.

air out the preposition "out" is sometimes added in NE expression "to air out" (one's views). In BE, the preposition is absent.

aircraft this noun is often used in the plural with -s in NE, e.g. "It is very sad that Nigerian Airways which had over twenty aircrafts in its fleet some years ago, today boasts of only one aircraft"; "Many aircrafts belonging to privately owned airlines are old." This noun is never found with the plural -s in BE. (Also in WAE).

Ajuwaya /adʒʊwaja/ often found in the register of Nigerian army, particularly in the context of military parade, with the meaning "As you were."

akamu /akamʊ/ pap prepared from the maize or corn flour usually taken while hot. It is known as "ogi" among the Yoruba. (SL: Hausa).

akanwu /akanwʊ/ potash; salt-like substance used in food preparation, and in the production of gunpowder. Igbo speakers call it "akanwu"; Hausa speakers say "kanwa" while Yoruba speakers say "kaun". "Akanwu" is also used to facilitate the softening of certain food items such as beans, breadfruit, cow skin or "ponmo", etc. It is also believed to have some medicinal effects. (SL: Hausa).

akara /akara/ bean cake; cake made from ground beans, duly seasoned and fried in hot oil. It is prepared by mixing bean flour with spices and salt. (SL: Yoruba).

akpu /akpʋ/ cassava tuber or plant (of Manihot esculenta; Manihot utilissima) mashed cassava, soaked in water for up to four days, washed clean, and cooked; foofoo; tapioca, or dried thinly-shredded cassava slices, e.g. "Give me akpu with egusi soup." (SL: Igbo).

akpuruka /akpʋrʋka/ "fake products" or "illegal transactions", as in "Someone helped me to send the fax by akpuruka way." This loanword is also frequently heard in the register of passengers who travel by luxury buses where "akpuruka" refers to the old brand of luxury buses while "concord" refers to the new brand of luxury buses. (SL: Igbo).

aku-uka /akʋ ʋka/ title for the traditional ruler of Wukari, as in "The Aku-Uka of Wukari.

akwete /akwete/ a type of cloth colourfully embroidered (SL: Igbo?).

Alaafin /ala:fi/ title for the traditional ruler of Oyo, as in "The Alaafin of Oyo." SL: Yoruba).

Aladura /aladura/ a religious sect associated with white gown. (SL: Yoruba).

Alhaji /alahadʒi/ title for a Muslim (usually a man), who has been to Mecca on holy pilgrimage. The title "Alhaji" is usually prefixed to a personal name and is seen to carry a social prestige, as in "Alhaji Shehu". This is an Arabic term that has come to NE via Hausa. Its female counterpart is alhaja or hajia. (SL: Arabic).

Alkali /alkali/ a magistrate or judge in an Islamic court. (SL: Arabic).

all many speakers of NE often use double adverbial for emphasis, as in "All he has to do is just leave the job." The use of double adverbial such as "all" and "just" would not be encountered very often in BE.

all what often used for "all that" or "what", as in "All what I have been saying is that he must pack out of my house" for BE "All that I have been saying is that he must pack out of my house" or "What I have been saying is that he must pack out of my house."

all in all this expression is often used in NE to mean "very powerful", as in "The Head of State is all in all." In BE, "all in all" means "when everything is considered", as in "All in all, the study tour has been a great success."

Allah /aːla/ the Islamic term for God. It is often used as an exclamation to mean "by God" e.g.
A: Are you sure you will hand over power to a democratically elected government?
B: Allah, I will.
(SL: Arabic).

alligator pepper a coinage for malagrotta pepper used mainly for eating kola nut, particularly among the Igbo people of Nigeria.

allottees refers to "those who have had portions of land allotted to them", e.g. "The approach allowed the allottees to bear the cost of infrastructure and other facilities." This word is derived in analogy with similar English words.

almajiri /almadʒiri/ "street urchins". The term is today synonymous with "street begging", particularly in cities in northern Nigeria. It frequently refers to a large number of school-age children, poorly clothed, poorly fed, and each clutching a medium-sized dish or plate and roaming the streets soliciting alms, e.g. "There is no doubt in my mind that the tens of thousands of almajiris up north who represent the expendable elements of combustion in any form of civil unrest, would not shy away from any opportunity to live a normal life." (SL: Hausa).

almanac an almanac in Nigerian context serves the same purpose as a calendar in British context. A Nigerian almanac usually contains several pictures of leaders or important members of the government, clubs, unions, etc. often displayed in the living rooms.

alphabet used to mean "letters of the alphabet" e.g. "My son now knows some English alphabets." This word is rarely plural in BE except in reference to two or more languages, e.g. "Our lecturer suggested that we should identify the differences and similarities between

Igbo and English alphabets."

Amadioha /amadiɔha/ god of thunder; its shrine is marked by a forked stick, or a log resting on two large bamboo posts; carved figure of god, e.g. "The elders invoked the spirit of Amadioha to destroy all the enemies of our village." (SL: Igbo).

amala /amala/ brown-coloured food prepared from yam flour, popular among the Yoruba. (SL: Yoruba).

Amanyanabo /amanjanabɔ/ title for the traditional ruler of Opobo, as in "Amanyanabo of Opobo." (SL: Opobo).

amebo /amibɔ/ one who interferes in other people's affairs. It can mean gossip or one that gossips, e.g. "Amebo, I didn't ask you" for BE "Gossip, I didn't ask you." (SL: Edo).

amend some users of NE, especially at the lower educational level often confuse "amend" with "mend", e.g. "I gave my torn trousers to the tailor to amend and he ended up destroying it." BE speakers will always use "mend" in this context.

amirul hajj /amiru ha:dʒ/ the leader of federal government delegation to Saudi Arabia on holy pilgrimage, e.g. "While submitting the report, the Amirul Hajj and Sultan of Sokoto, Alhaji Mohammadu Maccido, said that the 1998 pilgrimage was very well-organized, adding that airlifting ended three days before the closure of the Jeddah airport." (SL: Arabic).

among in NE, it functions either as a preposition or as an adverb, as in "He was not among." In BE, it functions only as a preposition, e.g. "I was among the crowd."

amount often used as an ellipsis for "amount of money", as in "What is the amount?" This usage is absent in BE. (also in WAE).

amusu /amusu/ It is commonly used by the Igbo to refer to the act of witchcraft or to one who is engaged in witchcraft. (SL: Igbo).

ankara /ankara/ wax print, as in "The ankaras were distributed free of charge to civil servants in the state by the state military administrator."

anniversary "one year" often collocates redundantly with "anniversary" in NE, as in "Both Ekwueme and Mallam Ciroma spoke at a public lecture organized to mark the one year anniversary of PDP at the International Conference Centre." This collocation does not occur in BE because "anniversary" denotes a date that is exactly one year after an event.

answer often used to mean "Be called"; "His/her name is", as in "She answers Ngozi" for BE "She is called Ngozi" or "Her name is Ngozi."

any complain? this is a question that is sometimes heard in NE especially by less educated persons for BE "Any problem?" or "Any complaint?"

anyhow stupidly, foolishly, e.g. "She talks anyhow" for BE "She talks stupidly."

---

any-load one who carries load for people for some money, commonly used in Edo and Delta states, e.g. "Please call any-load for me."

anything often used as a polite way of responding to a question proposing an offer, instead of being specific, e.g.
A: What can I offer you?
B: Anything.
BE speakers prefer to be specific to such a question.

APC an abbreviation for Arewa People's Congress, a socio-cultural organization, which seeks to prevent disunity among the various ethnic groups, that make up the north.

Apo Mansion /apo mænʃn/ the official residence of the Nigerian Senate President.

apollo conjunctivitis; an epidemic infection often characterized by the swelling of the eye, as in "I have apollo" for BE "I am suffering from conjunctivitis."

APP an abbreviation for All Peoples' Party, one of Nigeria's political parties.

applicant apart from its BE meaning, this term is also used for a jobless or unemployed person, as in "After five years of graduation from the university, she is still an applicant." In BE, "applicant" denotes a person who applies for something, e.g. for a job, a loan, etc. In NE, it denotes a social or occupational category, i.e. a class of young people who are still unemployed but are searching for jobs with the hope of being employed.

apply often used to mean "concern" or "have reference to", as in "My remark does not apply to you" for BE "My remark does not concern you."

appoint as the verb "appoint" is often followed by the preposition "as" in sentences where BE would consider this preposition to be redundant, e.g. "Dr. Olufemi has been appointed as the new head of department." Although the redundant usage of "as" is sometimes found in BE, many of its speakers would prefer to omit the preposition so that the above sentence becomes "Dr. Olufemi has been appointed the new head of department."

area boys a group of miscreants, especially in Lagos, as in "The area boys have blocked the road to Nnamdi Azikiwe Street."

are you a regularly heard question in NE is "Are you understanding me?" for BE "Do you understand me?"

arrangee often used to mean someone employed in illegal currency deals. It is derived in analogy with similar English words.

army often used as a clipped form of "in the army" as "My son is an army" instead of the more likely BE forms like "My son is a soldier" or "My son is in the army."

aroso /aroso/ a slang for a special brand of imported rice. This word is very commonly used among the Yoruba people, e.g. "We have ordered for two bags of aroso rice for our traditional wedding."

---

arrears in BE, this noun does not have a singular version and so takes the singular verb. In NE, it is sometimes found with the plural verb, e.g. "I didn't know that the arrears of the new minimum wage are as much as this."

ashewo /aʃewo/ a "prostitute" or a "flirt". This word is commonly used in NE to insult people especially women, so that one who is called "ashewo" may not be a prostitute, e.g. "Any man who thinks I can stay in the house while he roams about chasing every ashewo is mistaken." (SL: Yoruba).

Ashiwaju /aʃiwadʒu/ chieftaincy title; leader, as in "Ashiwaju Ilu", meaning "Leader of Ilu." (SL: Yoruba).

ask from this preposition sometimes follows "ask" in NE expressions where it will not be found in BE, as in "Ask from the chairman if there will be meeting next Sunday" for BE "Ask the chairman if there will be meeting next Sunday."

aso ebi /aʃɔ ebi/ an identical cloth worn by several persons, usually friends or relations, on a special occasion. (SL: Yoruba).

as of now many NE speakers use "as of now" where BE users would prefer "at the moment", e.g. "As of now, I have no job" for BE "At the moment, I have no job."

aso oke /aʃɔ oke/ a locally woven heavy wear worn by both men and women. It is commonly used for ceremonies such as wedding, burial, etc. (SL: Yoruba).

aso rock /asɔ rɔk/ the name for the presidential state house in Abuja.

ASP an abbreviation for the Assistant Supretendent of Police.

assassination frequently collocates with character, with the meaning "destruction of reputation", as in "Politicians have been advised to concentrate on issues rather than character assassination." This collocation is also found in BE but it does not occur as frequently as it does in NE.

assemble in NE, the word "together" often occurs after the verb "assemble" in contexts where it will not be found in BE, e.g. "The director asked me to assemble together all the necessary documents for today's meeting." In BE usage, "together" will be tautological in this sentence since it is already implied in the meaning of "assemble".

assignment frequently used in educational institutions where BE would prefer "homework", i.e. "a task imposed on students by their teacher" e.g. "Have you finished your assignment?" for "Have you finished your homework?" "Assignment" in BE means "a task or duty that is assigned to somebody", as in "She was sent abroad on an assignment for the Sunday Times."

assorted also known as "assorted meat", it refers to a mixture of different parts of meat usually served in restaurants, as in "In fact, many people derive great pleasure in requesting for these kinds of meat including assorted meat."

as such   often used as a conjunction to enhance meaning, as in "He cursed me, and as such, I beat him up." It is here used to mean "consequently", "as a result", "therefore". In BE, "as such" means "as the word is usually understood" or "in the exact sense of the word", e.g. "The new job is not a promotion as such, but it has good prospects."

as well as   in NE, this phrase is frequently used where BE would prefer "together with", e.g. "He took courses in history, sociology as well as psychology." Although both NE and BE employ this phrase with the meaning "in addition to", however, what follows it in BE is a fact which is assumed to be generally known, e.g. "During his five-year rule, the late Head of State took decisions alone, usurped judicial power as well as executive power." This means that in addition to the executive power which the Head of State or President is widely known to possess, he took decisions alone and usurped judicial power.

assure   this verb is strongly transitive in BE and is normally followed by an object in the form of a noun, a pronoun or a phrase, as in "They assured him of their willingness to work hard"; "He assured us that he will be here in good time." NE speakers sometimes use a "that" clause after this verb, e.g. "Omole assured that the university will continue to lay more emphasis on the welfare of both staff and students of this great institution"; "The Nigeria Deposit Insurance

---

Corporation (NDIC) weekend assured of the safety of funds belonging to deceased depositors in the 26 failed banks."

ASUU an acronym for the Academic Staff Union of Universities. It is often used to be synonymous with the university teacher, as in "These ASUU people do nothing but always want a salary increase."

at this preposition is often used in NE in positions where the BE would prefer "in", e.g. "When you get to Lagos, make sure you stay at my friend's house"; "There is a post office at Dugbe." In these two examples, "in" will be more likely to occur in BE.

at about at, e.g. "The meeting starts at about 4 o' clock" for BE "The meeting starts at 4 o' clock."

at my front this phrase is used where BE uses "in front of me", e.g. "Stand at my front" for BE "stand in front of me."

at par the phrase "at par with" meaning "equal in importance, quality, etc. to somebody/something" is found in NE where BE would prefer "on a par with", e.g. "Two students' essays are at par with each other" for BE "Two students' essays are on a par with each other."

at the rate of commonly used in the context of buying and selling to mean "at the price of..." or "for", as in "There is not much profit in this business because we buy these products at the rate of N50.00 each and sell at the rate of N55.00."

Atilogwu dancers /atilɔgwʊ dænsəz/ a popular traditional dancing group known for fast dancing steps and acrobatic displays; generic name for a family of festive dancers, marked by fast-paced rhythms, colourful costumes and vibrant dancing by young persons. (SL: Igbo).

atimes frequently written as one word in NE. In BE, it is usually written as two words, "at times", e.g. "The way those in government mismanage public fund atimes makes me feel that the future of the Nigerian youth is hopeless."

atmospheric condition of health sometimes used in letter writing in reference to state of health, e.g. "I hope you are in good atmospheric condition of health" for BE "I hope you are in good state of health."

a to! /a:to/ an exclamation expressing displeasure or indifference, commonly used by the Hausa. (SL: Hausa).

attachment ellipsis for "attachment seat"—a coinage in NE to describe makeshift seats or even standing positions in luxury buses, usually cheaper than the "main seat", e.g. "I don't want attachment. I want the main seat." "Attachment" also refers to the artificial hair, which women attach to their hair, and used in plaiting it.

August in BE, the collocation, "August visitor" is used in informal situations for humorous or ironic effects. In NE, it is regularly used in very formal occasions, e.g.

"I have the pleasure to introduce our august visitor to this august occasion."

August-break   this collocation is frequently used in NE to refer to a short dry weather known in meteorological parlance as "little dry season." It occurs within the third week of July and the first week of August, e.g. "The weather experts noted that rather than the August-break usually associated with the months of July and August following heavy rains, dull, cloudy and cold weather with little or no rainfall are presently being experienced by the public."

auntie   a respectful term for an older woman who may not be a close relative, e.g. "Please auntie, where can I get a bus to Oshodi?"; "Auntie Grace will soon be back from the market." In the second example, "auntie" is used as a title of respect usually prefixed to the name of a relative. See also "uncle".

ayaa!   /aja:/ an exclamation strongly expressing sympathy, used by the Hausa. (SL: Hausa).

B

ba? /baː/ Hausa equivalent of "abi"; that is, a way of confirming information which may be equivalent to "isn't it?", e.g.

A: You promised to assist me with some money today, ba Mallam?

B: Yes, but I have not received my salary. (SL: Hausa).

baale /baːle/ head of an extended family in Yorubaland. (SL: Yoruba).

baba /baba/ mode of an address or reference to a father, but often used as a respectful term of address to an older male who is not necessarily related to the speaker. (SL: Hausa and Yoruba).

babalawo /babalawo/ a traditional healer or diviner, as in "I know some people who claim to be Christians but always consult the babalawos"; "Obakhale was a traditional medicine practitioner otherwise known as babalawo." (SL: Yoruba).

babariga /babariga/ Hausa equivalent of "agbada", i.e. a big flowing gown, as in "Dressed in a light flowing babariga, the pro-democracy activist went straight to the head of the security team to register his displeasure at the manner the rally was disrupted." (SL: Hausa).

baby often used to refer to a female child as opposed to "boy", a male child.

Bachelors' eve a party organized on the eve of a wedding, usually by the friends and relations of the couple. In recent time, bachelors' eve can be held a week or two before the wedding.

back many users of NE use "at my back" where BE uses "behind me" e.g. "The lady standing at my back is my wife" for BE "The lady standing behind me is my wife."

backyard In BE, this would mean the area at the back of the house usually referred to as "the garden" or "business premises", "churchyards" or "dockyards". "Back yard" in NE means a piece of enclosed ground, usually at the back of a house, especially one surrounded by or attached to a building, often used for kitchen, gardening, rearing poultry, dumping garbage, etc., e.g. "Ensure that the backyard is swept every morning." It is also used as a vulgar expression to mean buttocks", as in "I like that girl but her backyard is flat" for BE "I like that girl but her buttocks are flat."

bad-boy a male criminal or a lawless and violent young man, e.g. "I suspect strongly that many bad-boys live in that house."

bad-eye "To look at someone with bad eye" suggests looking at someone with bad or evil intention.

bad heart often used as a NE idiomatic expression, among the less educated speakers, meaning "wicked", as in "You have a very bad heart" for BE "You are very wicked."

bad mouth used as an idiomatic expression in NE to mean "rude", "abusive" or "uncouth", especially, with the use of words, e.g. "Many children of this generation have bad mouth" for BE "Many children of this generation are rude."

bag "bagging" is used in NE where BE will prefer to use "obtaining" or "being awarded", e.g. "He left in search of the golden fleece in Vienna bagging three degrees in engineering." In BE, this verb is found only in informal contexts, particularly in the register of sports (especially of hunters) where "bag" means "kill" or "catch", as in "They bagged nothing except a couple of rabbits." But in NE, it is found in very formal contexts.

baggage never pluralized in BE where it means "personal belongings or possessions packed in cases, etc for traveling", but often pluralized in NE, as in "This bus cannot contain their baggages."

bahama low grass, usually planted on playgrounds, as in "After displaying unrehearsed acrobatics on the uneven bahama lawn outside, he ran back to his seat sweating all over as he vibrated with excitement."

bail in BE, "bail" means "money paid by or for somebody accused of a crime, as a guarantee that he will return for his trial if he is allowed to go free until then", as in "Bail was set at $1 million"; "The judge granted/refused to grant him bail." Besides the BE meaning, "bail" in the register associated with police means "bribe" or money paid so that one can be released from detention, as in "In fact, one man from whom a gun was also recovered was allowed to go scot-free after he bailed himself."

Bakassi Boys /bakasi bɔi:z/ unconventional anti-crime busters, who have their roots in Aba, and have now assumed the security outfit of most of the South Eastern states, but notorious for extra judicial killings of men suspected to be armed robbers, as in "Some of the legislators wanted the House to pass a motion asking the state government to set up a security outfit similar to Bakassi Boys in the East in Edo to contain the upsurge of armed robbers"; "Speaking on the state television, Dr. Mbadinuju said that the issue of invitation of Bakassi Boys to Onitsha has gone beyond himself as the governor stating that it is what the people want."

balance 1. as a verb, it means "complete payment of money", e.g. "Please have N10.00 now, I will balance you N3.00 in the evening."
2. it can be used as a noun with regards to complete payment or "change" (i.e. money returned to a customer), e.g. "I will come later for my balance" for "I will come later to collect my change." When this noun is used with reference to money in BE, it means "to compare the total amount of money gained and money spent in an account and record the sum needed to make them equal."
3. it is also often used as a verb with the meaning "sit

comfortably", e.g. "The driver urged everybody to balance properly before driving off." (Also in WAE).

bamboo the tree Bambusa vulgaris from which a variety of palm-wine and locally brewed gin known as kaikai are produced. Its leaves are used in roofing houses, especially in rural communities.

bamboo-bed bed made of bamboo.

bang slang commonly used among students meaning "to have sex", as in "I banged hell out of her" for "I had sex with her violently."

banga /banga/ a kind of soup popular among the Urhobo, as in "banga soup". (SL: Urhobo).

bar beach name for Lagos' most popular stretch of coastline.

barb in NE, "to barb one's hair" has the same meaning as "to cut one's hair" in BE. "A barber" is used to refer to one who cuts peoples' hair, as in "This time, the barber was ordered to scrape off every strand of hair on my head." But there is no verb as "barb" in BE. The verb "barb" is derived in analogy with existing forms whose nouns are formed by adding –er.

barrack 1. The form "barrack" is often used as a noun in NE for BE "barracks". "Barracks" is the form for both singular and plural, referring to a large building or a group of buildings for soldiers to live in. It is common in Nigeria to hear such statements as "He went to the barrack"; "There is a big barrack around us." The singular form "barrack" is found in BE as a verb, meaning "to shout criticism or protests at players in a game, speakers at a meeting, performers, etc.", e.g. "The crowd started barracking the team."

2. the collocations "military barracks", "police barracks" are found in NE where the qualifiers are redundant. The use of these qualifiers is to differentiate barracks occupied by soldiers from barracks occupied by the police, e.g. "I found many Yoruba people in a military barracks there."

basket used as a unit of measurement, as in "Small size of basket of tomatoes is currently at N500.00, the biggest basket at N1,000.00."

Basorun /baʃɔrʊ/ a popular chieftaincy title in Yorubaland often prefixed to the name of the title holder, e.g. "Basorun Abiola".

bawoni? /bawoni/ a common greeting for "How are you?" commonly used by the Yoruba. (SL: Yoruba).

be able "be able" is often used in collocation with "can" or "cannot" in NE where BE would consider its use redundant, e.g. "Only a strong military ruler can be able to probe past military regimes"; "I cannot be able to come tomorrow." In both examples, a BE speaker will omit "be able".

be fast now this expression is frequently heard in NE where BE would prefer to say "Don't waste the time" or "Do that work very quickly."

be going there is the tendency to prefer this progressive form in NE to the BE simple form, "go" e.g. Please settle

me and let me be going" for BE "Please settle me and let me go."

be with this idiomatic device is often preferred in NE, e.g. "Your pen is with me" where BE will prefer "I have your pen" or "I am in possession of your pen."

beat in BE, "beat" is used in the sense of hitting somebody or something hard repeatedly, especially with a stick or the hand. In NE, "beat" is frequently used in collocation with rain to denote "fall on", e.g. "Were you beaten by the rain?"

because there is a strong tendency in NE to produce tautological forms in constructions involving "because", e.g. "The reason is because I am poor." The word "because" is superfluous in this example.

become somebody sometimes used in NE to mean "become successful", as in "He will become somebody in future" for BE "He will become successful in future."

bed-sheet equivalent to the BE "sheet", e.g. "The bed-sheets should be washed, at least, once a week." (Also in WAE and in AmE).

been-to refers to one who has returned to Nigeria from a stay overseas, especially to Europe or North America, and who still exhibits some foreign idiosyncrasies. It is now obsolete and when used, it is slightly derogatory, as in "He still has not shedded off his been-to mentality from the US." It was commonly used up to the 1960s when to have "been-to" Britain or USA was highly admired. (Also in WAE).

beer parlour equivalent to BE "public house", i.e. a house or enclosure where beer is sold to customers for drinking on the premises.

before often used to indicate time measured back to a point in the past, e.g. "I'm shocked to hear that he is dead. We were together in a meeting two weeks before." BE would prefer "ago" to "before" in this sentence.

before-before a reduplicative form colloquially used in NE, especially at the lower educational level to mean "In the past"; "previously", as in "Before- before, 100 Naira was big money" for BE "In the past, 100 Naira was big money." (SL: Pidgin).

beg commonly used to mean "plead with", but "begging" attracts more sympathy and may often lead to forgiveness. "Begging" is sometimes dramatized by prostration and weeping in order to show remorse, e.g. "Please help me to beg the Head of State to forgive me." The BE meaning of "beg", i.e. "ask for" is too weak to express the NE sense of "beg."

belgium a coinage for imported used goods. The choice for "Belgium" may be because most imported second hand items come through Belgium, e.g. "One of my friends bought a big belgium fridge for only N10,000.00."

bend-down boutique often found in the register of buying and selling to refer to second hand or used wears, e.g. "I bought this bag from bend-down boutique." See also "okirika" and "tokunbo".

Benin /binin/ a city in Nigeria historically popular as a kingdom, from 1400 to 1600, famous for its brass, bronze and ivory sculptures. Benin is today the capital of Edo State.

bennisees the seed of Sesamum radiatum, used for its valuable oil called 'sesame oil', which is used for cooking, and for soap, lighting or fuel.

between in BE, this preposition is used in the period of time separating two days, years, events, etc. and linked with the conjunction "and", e.g. "It's cheaper to make international calls between 9 p.m. and 2 a.m."; "I'm usually free between Thursday and Saturday." In NE, the preposition "to" is sometimes used to link the two periods after "between", as in "Obi, who first cut his teeth in the profession with defunct Guardian Express between 1986 to 1988 was picked up on May 4, 1995 for publishing the story, "Col. Shuaibu: The man who betrayed coup suspects"."

Biafra /biafra/ name for the Eastern part of Nigeria that attempted to secede in a civil war from 1967 to 1970, e.g. "The former Biafran leader has been in the political limelight, campaigning for the Igbos to take the first shot at the presidency in the next political dispensation."

big often collocates with the verb "talk" meaning "intended to make an impression", as in "He likes talking big, but I know he's not that rich."

big-big a reduplicative form colloquially used in NE,

especially at the lower educational level of NE to describe "many big things", as in "In his village, there are big-big houses." (SL: Pidgin).

big chic often used to refer to comfortable young women (particularly single women), e.g. "Joy is a big chic. She now lives in a duplex in Lagos."

bigman refers to a wealthy man, an influential man or a highly placed person, as in "Only bigmen can buy a land in Abuja." There is also bigmanism, i.e. the act of being and/or behaving like a bigman.

big problem serious problem, e.g. "I have a big problem" for BE "I have a serious problem."

bigwoman refers to a wealthy woman, an influential woman or a highly placed woman, e.g. "She has suddenly become a bigwoman by flirting with politicians." There is also bigwomanism, i.e. the act of being and/or behaving like a bigwoman.

biko /biko/ "please" commonly used among the Igbo, as in "Biko can you do me a favour?" (SL: Igbo).

birds of the same feather "The same feather" replaces "a feather" in NE idiomatic expression "birds of the same feather (flock together)" which is equivalent to BE "birds of a feather (flock together)", i.e. People of the same kind (often bad) like each other's company. E.g. "I'm not surprised that Chike and Andrew are such close friends; they're birds of the same feather" for BE "I'm not surprised that Chike and Andrew are such close friends; they're birds of a feather."

bite "finger" substitutes for "hand" in the NE idiomatic expression "bite the finger that feeds one" which is equivalent to BE "bite the hand that feeds one", meaning "harm somebody who has been kind to one", e.g. "Dipo, I can't believe that you're now biting the finger that fed you" for "Dipo, I can't believe that you're now biting the hand that fed you."

bitter-kola a particular brand of kola nut that is usually bitter and different from kola nut. (See kola-nut).

bitterleaf the green bitter vegetable of Vernonia anyadalina, the leaves of which are thoroughly washed and used for cooking soup, thus "bitterleaf soup". It is also used as a herb and believed to possess anti-hypertensive properties.

black axe a coinage for a secret cult popular on university campuses.

black and white 'write' often collocates with 'black and white' in NE but not in BE expressions, e.g. "Can you write that down in black and white?" for BE "Can you put that down in black and white?" or "Can you write that down?"

black in complexion many speakers of NE use "black in complexion" for "dark-skinned", e.g. "He is black in complexion" for BE "He is dark-skinned."

blackman formed in agglutination for BE 'black man'.

black market "parallel market", e.g. "Although the official value of one US dollar is N112.00, it is sold for

N135.00 in the black market."

black pepper a spice with pungent taste botanically known as Piper Guineense. This spice is very rich in essential oils. It is believed to have medicinal values.

black soap soap made of palm-oil or palm-kernel oil or coco-nut oil and burnt ashes of palm leaves, believed to have medicinal effect.

blade a clipped form for "razor-blade", as in "Do you have blade?"

bloody civilian a collocation , often derogatory, frequently used by military personnels to insult or rebuke non-military persons, e.g. "The ex-MILAD, who was promoted from Colonel to Brigadier-General few days to the end of the last military regime, has since then been living in Kaduna as a bloody civilian."

blue a colourant in form of powder usually blue, often mixed in water and applied to a white material to reduce the whiteness of the colour.

bluff it is also used to mean "to show off", besides its BE meaning, as in "He is always bluffing in public" for BE "She is always showing off in public."

bo /buo/ a loanword for "please", as in "Leave me alone bo" for BE "Please leave me alone"; "Don't disturb me bo" for BE "Please don't disturb me." (SL: Pidgin).

bobo /bɔbɔ/ often used to refer to a young man, as in "This bobo is simply unstoppable."

---

bolekaja /bɔlekadʒa/ a small bus used for transportation, popular among the Yoruba. "Bolekaja" means "come down, let us fight", and this bus is so-named because it is always full, and one needs to be aggressive to get in. "Bolekaja" is today associated with aggressiveness so that one can talk of "bolekaja diplomacy", meaning aggressive diplomacy, as in "Ikimi is the progenitor of what has now become bolekaja diplomacy." (SL: Yoruba).

boli /bɔli/ roasted plantain. (SL: Yoruba).

bolted away the particle 'away' often collocates with 'bolt' in NE in contexts where it will not be found in BE, e.g. "The convict has bolted away from the prison cell" for BE "The convict has bolted from the prison cell", where it means 'run away'.

bom-boy /bɔmbɔi/ often used by the less educated NE speakers to refer to 'boy-child', as in "Papa bom-boy", i.e. "the father of a boy-child" or "the father of a male child." (SL: Pidgin).

bone-to-bone a slang commonly used by students to describe a dance in which a man dances with another man, as in "The girls we invited for the party did not come, and so we had to dance bone-to-bone."

bonga fish a species of dried fish which is often thin-shaped. It can be used metaphorically, e.g. "The girl is a bonga fish" for BE "The girl is very thin."

borrow 1. this term is often used in extended sense (particularly by those with inadequate exposure to

English) to cover the meaning of BE "lend", e.g. "I want you to borrow me some money. I will pay back tomorrow."
2. in the students' register, 'borrow a course' is frequently used for BE 'take a course', as in "The course I borrowed from English department was not computed in my result" for BE "The course, which I took from English department was not computed in my result."

both often followed by the negative form of a verb, e.g. "Both of them did not visit me." BE would normally prefer a construction with the negative adjective or pronoun to the use of verb followed by the negative form of the verb, so that the NE example above will be equivalent to BE "Neither of them visited me."

bottom power a practice in which women use sex to influence favours from men, as in "An actress has deployed a situation where many ladies use bottom power to get into the film industry."

boubou /bubu/ free flowing big gown worn by women, e.g. "Our source told us that it was because of the pregnancy that Aunty Lola always adorns different types of boubou or kaftan with kampala or tie and dye fabrics."

bow-leg of legs, slightly curved, e.g. "James has bow-legs."

boy apart from its BE meaning, it is also used to refer to a male servant or apprentice of whatever age, as in "I have been staying in my bookshop since this year because my boys have become very dishonest."

BP an abbreviation for blood pressure often used to refer to high blood pressure, e.g. "Is it true that BP leads to a stroke?"

brace up the particle "up" often follows "brace" in NE where it does not occur in BE, e.g. "The city was bracing up for the expected arrival of fighters who launched a rebellion against Kabila earlier this month." The occurrence of this particle in this context will be considered redundant in BE.

branch frequently used to mean "stop on one's way to somewhere else", that is, "to stop over", e.g. "I came late because I branched to my uncle's house."

breadfruit a big ball-like fruit containing small seeds which are usually fried or cooked and eaten as food, particularly by the Igbo.

break and pay this is a notice of warning in some public houses such as hotels and drinking houses that customers who break glasses or plates will be asked to pay for them.

break one's head an idiomatic expression, e.g. "I have been breaking my head trying to remember what he told me." This idiom is absent in BE, and may be equivalent to "rack one's brains", i.e. "to try very hard to think of something or remember something", e.g. "We racked our brains for an answer."

bride-price dowry or money which a man pays to the

parents of a girl whom he wishes to marry, as in "I have indeed terminated the marriage and you may keep the bride price if you like." (Also in WAE).

bring money an imperative expression commonly heard in the register of buying and selling to indicate an acceptance by the seller of a price offered by the buyer, e.g.:
Buyer: How much for your mangoes?
Seller: Five naira each.
Buyer: What of three for ten naira?
Seller: Bring money.
BE has no exact equivalent of this expression since the type of haggling that results in this expression is absent in the context of buying and selling in Britain.

Broken an ellipsis for "Broken English", i.e. incorrect English; a term which is commonly used to refer both to Pidgin and to sub-standard forms of English. Often used as a noun, e.g. "Most people in Lagos and Port Harcourt speak only Broken."

brokered frequently used as a verb in NE e.g. "The Liberian peace talk was brokered by Nigeria." The BE version of it would probably be "The Liberian peace talk was held with Nigeria acting as a broker."

brother the term "brother" may be used to include one's half brother, uncle, cousin, kinsman, or a male relation of the same generation depending on the context. It can also be used as a term of respect for an elder brother or even an older man who is not one's relation, e.g. "Brother, please give me some money." When prefixed to a name, it is also intended as a form of respect, as in "Brother Emeka." Similarly, "brother"/ "sister" is also used by the Pentecostal churches in Nigeria, with the meaning "brother/sister in Christ." In BE, "brother" refers to child of the same parents. (Also in WAE).

brown beans distinctions are usually made between the two major varieties of beans, "white beans" and "red beans", as in "Beans has the same price at both markets, the brown beans is sold for N4,500.00 per bag while the white beans is sold for N4,300.00."

buba /buba/ a collarless short loose garment with ample sleeves reaching the elbow, worn mainly by women and sometimes by men. (SL: Yoruba).

bukateria /bukateriə/ a cheap eating place.

bungalow a "self-contained apartment" as opposed to a flat.

buns a ball of flour fried in groundnut oil.

burukutu /burukutu/ alcoholic drink distilled locally from guinea-corn or millet, e.g. "Details of the trip was actually revealed at the normal Thursday gathering in the most popular burukutu joint here in Jebba." (SL: Hausa).

bush frequently used in NE to refer to the interior or "rural area", as in "He comes from one of the bush areas of Igboland" for BE "He comes from one of the rural areas of Igboland." It is also used to refer to "forest" or uncultivated lands far from home, where hunting usually takes place, e.g. "He went to the bush."

bush allowance a slang, commonly used in schools and institutions of higher learning, to describe a situation where some male teachers indulge in sexual affairs with their female students, as in "Although teachers are poorly paid, they enjoy bush allowance."

bushfire "bushfire" often substitutes for "wild fire" in the NE idiomatic usage "spread like bushfire" which is equivalent to BE "spread like wild fire", meaning "(especially of rumours, reports or diseases) to spread among a group of people very quickly", e.g. "It is feared that if the society does not change its attitude toward sex, the dreaded Acquired Immune Deficiency Syndrome (AIDS) will spread across the country like a bushfire."

bushman often used to describe an uncivilized or naive person, as in "I am not surprised at his behaviour. He is a bushman." (Also in WAE).

bush meat this is roughly equivalent to BE "game", i.e. the meat of wild animals killed by hunters in the forest. Grasscutter, bush-pig, antelope, monkey are particularly popular kinds of bush meat, which is served in many eating places. (Also in WAE).

butter has an extended meaning which includes "margarine".

by in expressions of time, "by" is widely used where BE uses "at", e.g. "Expect me in your house by 5 o'clock." Also in the context of public transportation, "by" is frequently used in description of destination, so that when a commuter stops a taxi within Benin and tells the driver "New Benin by Mission Road", "by" here may be equivalent to "at the junction with."

C

cake NE uses the idiom "To eat one's cake and have it" as an inversion of BE "To have one's cake and eat it", meaning (usually in the negative sentences) "to enjoy the benefits from two different courses of action, etc. when only one or the other is possible", e.g. "She wants to pass the examination but doesn't want to read. She can't eat her cake and have it." In BE, the second sentence would be "She can't have her cake and eat it."

calabash a brown, dried and round-like fragile container made of the fruit of the calabash tree (Crescentia Cujete) used for storing palm-wine. The smaller ones are often used as cup for drinking palm-wine, kunu, burukutu, etc.

call often used to mean "name", e.g. "I have forgotten what they call the tree" for BE "I have forgotten the name of the tree"; "I think they call his first son Andrew" for "I think the name of his first son is Andrew."

camp a small settlement usually along the riverine.

CAN an acronym for Christian Association of Nigeria, as in "CAN wants religious crisis averted in Kwara."

canal-city an euphemism for Calabar, one of the cities

in the South South part of Nigeria.

canfor /kanfɔ/ small ball-like whitish substance, whose scent is believed to drive away insects from boxes and wardrobes.

cannot be possible 'cannot be' and 'possible' often collocate in NE where it will be considered tautological in BE, e.g. "That cannot be possible" for BE "That cannot be (so)" or "That is not possible."

canteen "canteen" in BE refers to a place where food and drink are served in a factory, an office, a school, etc. In NE, it often denotes a small, cheap eating place, usually in a makeshift accommodation.

canvas an ellipsis for "canvas shoes".

car is smoking popularly heard in reference to the engine of a car that produces some smoke, e.g. "Your car is smoking" for BE "The engine of your car is producing some smoke."

carpet commonly used for BE "linoleum" in rubber form. Users of NE frequently make distinctions between "carpet" and "rug". "Rug" is used in BE sense of "fitted carpet", i.e. carpet with measurements coinciding exactly with the length and breadth of a room.

care-less often used by the less educated speakers of NE as a verb, e.g. "I care-less about your traveling to Abeokuta", meaning "Your traveling to Abeokuta is none-of-my business." "Careless" functions as an adjective in BE, as in "a careless driver".

carelessly has an extended meaning when it collocates with the stative verbs "lie" or "sit", as in "That girl is always sitting carelessly." This sentence in NE is understood to mean that the girl in question is always sitting down in such a way that she exposes the private parts of her body. The sentence will not be understood in this sense in BE because "carelessly" does not usually collocate with stative verbs.

carry-over popularly used in higher educational institutions to refer to "the repeating of a course already taken and failed", as in "Three final year students are not graduating because they have carry-overs in some courses."

case get k-leg very serious, as in "The case has k-leg" for BE "The case is very serious."

cashew a small, pear-shaped, yellow fruit, carrying a brown crescent-shaped nut (cashew nut) on its bottom. The fruit is borne on a medium-sized tree (Anacardium occidentale), and cashew nuts are fried and eaten like groundnut. Its nut contains oil, which can cause blistering of the skin.

cash madam "an influential public woman", "a wealthy woman", e.g. "Who else, but a woman, can best relate with and understand the peculiar needs of these cash madams?"

cassava the tropical plant of manoic tapioca usually long, hard-fleshed and white inside. It is of two distinct types: Sweet cassava (Manihot dulcis), and bitter cassava

(Manihot esculenta or utilissima). The Sweet cassava is usually eaten as vegetable, and the root eaten boiled or roasted in some parts of the country, while the bitter cassava provides starch. The two varieties can be processed to produce garri, i.e. grated cassava fried to semi-coarse flour.

cassava-flour the meal of the grated bitter cassava from which the poisonous juice has been extracted by squeezing.

cassava-starch starch obtained by drying in the sun the poisonous juice of the grated bitter-cassava.

cassava-stick stick of cassava usually planted and harvested after some time.

cassette ellipsis for "radio-cassette", as in "My cassette is faulty" for BE "My radio-cassette is faulty."

catch 1. "to make a new catch" is a slang commonly used among students to mean "to have a new lover", as in "I stopped going out with my former girl-friend immediately I made a new catch."
2. often used in NE with the meaning "to arrest", as in "Police have caught two of the armed robbers who attacked our neighbours yesterday."

CBN an abbreviation for the Central Bank of Nigeria, the highest bank for the Federal Republic of Nigeria.

CCC an abbreviation for Celestial Church of Christ, one of the indigenous churches in Nigeria associated with the white garment and bare-footedness.

celebrant a person hosting a party or any social function is frequently addressed as the "celebrant", e.g. "May I invite the celebrant to give a vote of thanks." In BE, the term is used for a priest who conducts church service.

cell has the extended meaning of "prison", as in "A former Head of State is still in the cell."

CFR Commander of the Federal Republic—Nigeria's third highest honour, usually awarded to persons who have distinguished themselves in their chosen fields of endeavour.

CGS an abbreviation for the Chief of General Staff, who serves as the vice president under a military regime in Nigeria.

chairlady frequently used in NE to mean "chairwoman", as in "The chairlady for this occasion is Mrs. Debo."

chairman "chairman" is a noun in BE, but it is sometimes used in NE as a verb, e.g. "The person to chairman this occasion is no other person than the president himself"; "Last year's town union meeting was chairmaned by our traditional ruler."

chance 1. often used to mean "room" or "space", as in "Join the other bus. There is no more chance in this one." As a noun, "chance" in BE denotes possibility and opportunity and is never used in the context above. 2. chance is also often used in NE to mean "time", as in "I have no chance to reply to your letter" for BE "I have no time to reply to your letter."

charge NE frequently permits expressions such as "He was charged of murder"; "He was charged for stealing." In BE, one is usually charged "with".

chase a popular NE slang which means to "woo a person of the opposite sex for a casual relationship", as in "Our boss is a womanizer. He is always chasing his secretaries." "Chase" is not used when the intention of wooing a girl is marriage.

cheap often used by students to mean "not difficult" or "easy", e.g. "The paper was very cheap" for BE "The paper was very easy"; "I don't like going out with cheap girls" for BE "I don't like going out with flirts (i.e. girls that are easily wooed by men)."

check 1. visit, as in "Please try to check me this evening."
2. search or look for, as in "I have checked for the money everywhere, and did not find it."
3. in the register of buying and selling, "Come and check" is an invitation to a buyer to have a look round the store.

chei! /tʃei/ an exclamation expressing surprise. (SL: Igbo).

chewing-stick a fibrous piece of dried or fresh wood (often bitter) chewed at one end to soften it and used for cleaning the teeth. (Also in WAE)).

chi /tʃi/ a loanword for "one's own personal god", as in

"Their plan was to kill him but his chi did not allow them to succeed." (SL: Igbo).

chicken change "change" replaces "feed" in NE idiomatic expression "chicken change" which is equivalent to BE "chicken feed", i.e. a small unimportant amount of money. E.g. "Your salary is a chicken change compared to what I earn" for BE "Your salary is a chicken feed compared to what I earn."

chief a title indicating social recognition which is usually prefixed to the name of a person who has taken a traditional title as in "Chief Banjo". It is often used as an appellation by subordinates to address their boss or leader, e.g. "Has anyone seen Chief since this morning?" In BE, "chief" refers to head or senior member of an organization.

chief priest the owner of an oracle.

child's play the NE idiomatic expression, "a child's play" substitutes for BE's "child's play", e.g. "The football match is going to be a child's play." BE form of this idiomatic expression is without the indefinite article.

chin-chin small fried cakes usually hard, and commonly patronized by children and students, e.g. "The headmaster yesterday warned that, henceforth, pupils who steal some money from their parents to buy chin-chin will be punished."

Chineke /tʃineke/ "God." It is often used as an exclamation to express surprise, e.g.

A: I just heard in the news that Denmark defeated the Super Eagles by 4 goals to one.
B: Chineke! (SL: Igbo).

choke up commonly heard in educational institutions, meaning "too busy", e.g. "I will not be able to finish revising my note-books before the examination. I am already choked up by time."

chop commonly used colloquially with the following meanings:
1. as a noun, it means food, as in, "Bring my chop."
2. as a verb, it means "to eat", as in "Come and chop." (SL: Pidgin).

chop-money it means money that is meant for feeding, as in "Ever since he married a second wife, my husband has refused to give me chop-money."

chop one chop two snacks commonly found in schools.

clap frequently collocates with "for" in NE, as in "Clap for him." In BE, the preferred form is "Give him a clap."

clean commonly used in the register of writing and typing with the meaning "erase". "Clean it" is commonly heard where BE would prefer "Erase it". Similarly, "cleaner" in NE is equivalent to BE "eraser".

close the less educated speakers of NE often use this verb in collocation with "light" where BE uses "switch off" or "turn off". Thus, "Close the light" is equivalent to BE "Switch off/turn off the light." In the same vein, "Open the light" is equivalent to "Switch on/turn on the light." In BE, the verb "close/open" will collocate with door, booth, etc. but not with "the light".

clothes this NE construction "I have given him, at least, three of my clothes, this year alone" is not likely to be heard from a BE speaker who would prefer to use "items of clothing" or would specify the garments.

co-wife in Nigeria where polygamy is permitted, the term "co-wife" is often used to mean "other wife", as in "This is my husband's co-wife" meaning "This is my husband's other wife."

coal-city an euphemism for Enugu, a city famous for the production of coal.

cockroach this is the name of a voracious insect common in tropical regions but it is often used as a slang by students to refer to one who studies late at night because of the belief that cockroaches don't sleep at night, as a nocturnal insect.

coconut the tree Cocos nucifera (Palmae) that produces a fruit whose nut is cracked and eaten.

coconut-head used idiomatically to mean unintelligent; one who finds it difficult to understand things, as in "You have a coconut-head."

• **coconut-oil** oil used for cooking or for cosmetic use, produced domestically by squeezing or boiling ground coconut.

coconut-rice rice prepared by adding the water or oil squeezed out from ground coconut. This gives it the special coconut flavour.

coconut-water the tasty liquid contained inside the coconut. It is a refreshing drink, which is often believed to have medicinal value.

cocoyam an edible plant and its tuber, smaller in size than yam or cassava.

cold water water that is stored in the fridge, e.g. "Can I have a glass of cold water?"

collection an ellipsis for "a collection of photographs" or an "album", e.g. "Your collection is very rich." This sense is lacking in BE where the likely utterance would be "Your collection of photographs is rich."

colonial masters used in reference to the British and other European countries that colonized African countries, e.g. "The colonial masters imposed their language and culture on the indigenous peoples of Africa."

colonial mentality a commonly used collocation meaning "conservative", "unprogressive", as in "Colonial mentality is our problem in this country. Otherwise, why should anyone prefer fake foreign goods to the superior locally made goods?" It is frequently used with reference to attitudes, which tend to suggest the superiority of the white man, or of imported goods.

coloured TV in NE, "coloured TV/television" is commonly used for BE "colour TV set/television"; i.e. a television set which transmits in colour, as in "The controversial custom-made coloured television sets ordered last year by ABG Communications to facilitate the late General Sani Abacha`s self-succession bid to presidency is now being distributed to the various state governments for sale to civil servants."

come... "come" is often used, especially by journalists to precede a future date as a reference to an event that is to happen, e.g. "Come Saturday, November 19, the man who has dominated Nigerian politics for over six decades will be laid to rest." "Come Saturday, November 19" is equivalent to BE "On Saturday, November 19" or "When Saturday, November 19 comes."

come again   in BE, this usage means "to return". In NE, it means "to repeat". It is also informally used to ask the question "What did you say?" e.g. "Please come again" is equivalent to BE "Please repeat" or "What did you say?"

come and eat   this expression is frequently heard in NE as a polite way of inviting a guest to share some food with his host. In this context, a BE speaker may use the expression "Would you mind our eating together?"

come today come tomorrow delays, disappointments, as in "I hope it will be ready tomorrow because I don't like come today come tomorrow" for BE "I hope it will be ready tomorrow because I don't like disappointments."

combat   the verb, "combat", i.e. "to try to reduce or

---

destroy something" is sometimes followed by the preposition "against", e.g. "The state government has been trying to combat against the outbreak of infectious diseases." BE uses this verb without the preposition.

commission also known as "kick-back", "commission" is frequently used in the register of political administration to mean "bribe", e.g. "Each contract specified a commission to be paid to a specific beneficiary." In BE, "commission" stands for an amount of money paid to somebody for selling goods, which increases with the quantity of goods sold.

common entrance examination often shortened to "common entrance" or "entrance", it is a competitive examination for children in the final stage of their primary education for selection into public secondary schools.

common man this word in BE means "average" or "ordinary" citizens. In NE, it means the "the downtrodden", e.g. "The politicians are only interested in their pockets and are never bothered about the plight of the common man."

competent constructions in which "competent" collocates redundantly with "enough" are often heard in NE, e.g. "The Assistant Police Commissioner stated that he was not competent enough to speak on that matter." In BE, "enough" will be considered redundant in this sentence since "competent" sufficiently expresses the implied meaning.

complete this verb is frequently used to collocate with "money", as in "The money is not complete. It remains N4.00." This utterance may be said by a creditor to a debtor when the former feels that the later still has to give him N4.00. Complete is also sometimes used emphatically in NE where it may not be found in BE, e.g. "He has not eaten beef for complete one year" for BE "He has not eaten beef for one year."

compound frequently used in NE to refer to an area surrounded by different buildings belonging to an extended family, as in "Chief Ohia's compound". As in BE, it can also refer to a big space of land belonging to a school, a church, etc, as in "school compound", "prison compound", etc.

comprise some speakers of NE use the preposition "of" to follow "comprise", perhaps in analogy with "consist of", as in "He pledged that the new cabinet will comprise of men of integrity from diverse ethnic and ideological backgrounds." BE usage would be without the preposition, e.g. "The flat comprises two bedrooms, a kitchen and a bathroom"; "Two small boys and a dog comprised the street entertainer's only audience."

CON Commander of the Order of the Niger—Nigeria's fourth highest national honour usually awarded to persons who have distinguished themselves in their chosen career.

concubine often used to mean a woman with whom a married man is having an affair outside his marriage. It may be equivalent to the BE "mistress".

condemned "be condemned" is equivalent in meaning to "be no longer useful" or "out of use", e.g. "All the trousers under the bed are condemned." In BE, apart from the legal register where this verb frequently occurs, as in "He was found guilty and therefore condemned to death", it is also used with the meaning "criticise", "show disapproval", e.g. "We all condemned him for his mistake." The NE extension is not found in BE.

condole used transitively in NE where 'with' is omitted, e.g. "He has already written to condole his friend on the death of his mother" for BE "He has already written to condole with his friend on the death of his mother."

congo meat delicacy prepared from snails, popular in the southern part of Nigeria.

congratulate in NE, this verb is often followed by the preposition "for", as in "We went to congratulate him for his recent promotion." This verb is followed by the preposition "on" in BE, e.g. "We congratulated her on her new job"; "My dad was the first to congratulate me on my thirtieth birthday."

contest for often formed in analogy with 'vie for', 'compete for', etc. with the addition of 'for' in NE which is unnecessary in BE, e.g. "Two ministers were dropped from the cabinet because of their alleged intention to contest for the governorship of their states" for BE "Two ministers were dropped from the cabinet because of their alleged intention to contest the governorship of their states."

convertees "proselytes", i.e. those who have been converted to a new faith, as in "All the convertees are expected to wait behind the pastor's office for a special prayer." This word is not found in BE.

cool down calm down; take it easy, e.g. "cool down; we will solve your problem" for BE "Calm down; we will solve your problem."

cope up with many NE speakers insert the particle "up" after "cope" where BE speakers would consider the use of this particle as redundant, as in "I don't know how to cope up with all these problems." BE uses either "cope" or "cope with", e.g. "She recently lost her job and had to withdraw her children from school, so it's not surprising that she can't cope"; "The roads simply can't cope with all the traffic now using them."

corner the noun "corner" substitutes for "cranny" in the NE idiomatic usage "every nook and corner" which is equivalent to BE "every nook and cranny", i.e. "every part of a place", as in "Good footballers abound in every nook and corner of this country."

corper an ellipsis for a member of the National Youth Service Corps (NYSC), e.g. "She is a corper."

correct 1. a NE way of describing one as a fool, a daft, or mad is evident in the collocation of this word with the negative morpheme "not" and the noun "head", as in "Your head is not correct." In BE, "correct" can collocate with "time", "dress", etc. but not with "head". 2. the meaning of "correct" is often used to include

---

"mark", as in "Please sir, have you finished correcting our examination papers?"

costly more commonly used in NE than in BE, where "dear" is more colloquially used with the meaning "expensive", e.g. "Meat was very costly last Friday, probably because of Sallah celebration." BE will prefer "dear" to "costly" in this sentence.

co-tenant a tenant who lives in the same house with another tenant is said to be his "co-tenant" in NE, e.g. "A friend of mine once told me that he'd slept with all three young daughters of his landlord and another daughter of a co-tenant."

cottonseed the material found after removing the lint and fuzz in cotton; it is frequently used for consumption in soups and stews, and also for animal feeds. It is often processed to produce cottonseed oil, which is consumed as vegetable oil.

could many speakers of NE often tend to use the past tense form "could" where BE speakers would prefer "can", as in "I could remember that he was here last week"; "Try to be here before 6 a.m. so that we could leave very early"; "We could succeed in our business if we are lucky." In BE, "could" may be used to indicate "ability", as in "He couldn't answer the questions."

coupist someone who was involved in coup d'etat, e.g. "Such were the fortunes of the country since the pioneer coupist opened the floodgate of military coups on January 15, 1966."

countryman refers to "a person from one's own town or ethnic group" in NE usage as opposed to "person from one's own country" in BE usage. The use of this word is common among the less educated speakers of NE. It has become obsolete in BE where the phrase "fellow countrymen" is still used.

country-people "compatriots" or "fellow country men."

coupion /kupiɔn/ a type of lace material popular among Nigerian men and women. There is also a "baby coupion", which is simpler in design and therefore cheaper, as in "He bought coupion for his girlfriend and bought a baby coupion for his wife."

cover-cloth a long piece of cloth wrapped around the body or to cover the body and used for sleeping, and for relaxing in the house.

cow-meat less educated Nigerians prefer to refer to "beef" as "cow-meat."

cow-tail delicacy with a lot of spices made of cow-tail meat.

crack jokes used where BE will use "make jokes", e.g. "Ibe often cracks jokes when serious matters are discussed."

crack one's brain equivalent to BE "rack one's brain", meaning "make great mental effort", as in "I have been busy since morning cracking my brain over that question." See also "break one's head."

---

cram frequently used in NE to mean "learn by heart", e.g. "I simply crammed the teacher's note to be able to pass the examination." "Cramming" is also used in NE outside the examination context, as in cramming the quotations in the Bible or in Shakespeare's plays. "Cram" is used in BE in informal style to denote "to learn a lot of facts in a short time, especially for an examination", as in "Emma passed his examination after just one week's cramming."

craw-craw equivalent to "scabies", e.g. "The craw-craw on your hands is enough pollution already."

credit often used by students to mean "pass with credit" or "have a credit in", e.g. "I did not credit my English" for BE "I did not have a credit in English."

cup 1. "cup" in BE denotes "a small container shaped like a bowl, usually with a handle, used for drinking tea, coffee, etc." In NE, "cup" is often used also for "glass", "tumbler", as in "Can I have a cup of water?" for BE "Can I have a glass of water?"
2. a popular NE expression is "His/her cup is full", meaning "His/her sins are too many", e.g. "His cup is getting filled much faster and there seems to be no other place for the cheat to hide."

cushion-chair "chair with cushions", it is equivalent to BE "armchair".

customer in NE, customer can denote either the buyer or the seller in a market transaction. "Meeting my customer" means meeting the person from whom I normally buy things. In BE, "customer" denotes only the buyer.

cut the substitution of the definite article "the" for an indefinite article "a" is found in the NE idiomatic expression "to cut the long story short" which is equivalent to BE "to cut a long story short", i.e. "to get to the point of what one is saying quickly."

cycle "cycle" sometimes substitutes for "circle" in the NE idiomatic usage "vicious cycle" which is equivalent to BE "vicious circle", meaning "a continuing situation in which one problem or need leads to another and the new problem makes the first problem worse", e.g. "He needs much money to help his family out of poverty and without much money, he cannot help them—it's a vicious cycle."

D

dabaru /dabaru/ "spoil", "confuse", as in "Most Nigerians of Ph.D. status will use big big English to dabaru us to the point that we miss the message while trying to figure out the grammar." (SL: Pidgin/Yoruba?).

dada dreadlocks; also referred to as Rasterferri's hair, as in "What was considered unfashionable yesterday may well become the rave tomorrow, and so it was with dada or dreadlocks as the fashion pace setters call it."

daddy a respectful mode of address to a man who may not be one's father, as in "Daddy, come and buy rice from me."

daily-paid "a daily-paid worker" refers to someone who works and gets his remuneration on daily basis as opposed to a regular staff in an establishment.

dandoko /dandoko/ a carrier or potter. (SL: Hausa).

dane gun short gun manufactured by the village blacksmith, and fired with gun powder, e.g. "It was the replica of my grand father's dane gun, only much much smaller."

danfo /danfo/ a small passenger-carrying bus. "Danfo" is different from the luxury bus and "molue" because it is the smallest of the three passenger-carrying buses.

danfo-wagon /danfo wægɔn/ a bus whose body is built of wood. It is also known as "wole-wole", a loanword for passenger-bus (SL: Yoruba).

danshiki /danʃiki/ a sleeveless jumper, i.e. gown with wide armpits and reaches to the knees, commonly worn by men, e.g. "The popularity of danshiki among the young men today attests to its quality." (SL: Hausa).

dash 1. as a verb, it means "give" or "give out", as in "Please uncle, dash me some money" for BE "Please uncle, give me some money." When used in this sense, it has the same meaning as "to tip".
2. as a noun, it means "gift" or "free", as in "I don't think I can do this job for dash" for BE "I don't think I can do this job free of charge." (SL: Pidgin).

day many speakers of NE say "day before yesterday" where BE speakers use "the day before yesterday", e.g. "I came back only day before yesterday" for BE "I came back only the day before yesterday."

day in, day out often used in NE with the meaning "everytime", as in "I have been coming here day in, day out without meeting anybody." In BE, the expression "day in, day out" means "everyday without exception", e.g. "Day in, day out, no matter what the weather is like, she walks ten miles."

days NE uses the plural form of "day" in the phrase "in one's days" as an equivalent of BE "in one's day" i.e. during one's life; in a period of success, wealth, power, etc, e.g. "Earnest Okonkwo was the best football commentator in his days." In this sentence, BE would use the singular form of "day".

dawadawa /dawadawa/ special spices more commonly used for cooking in northern Nigeria, e.g. "My husband likes jollof rice prepared with lots of dawadawa." (SL: Hausa).

dead wood this noun is often found in the plural form in NE expressions, e.g. "On the proposed rationalization in the civil service, the Minister of Labour stated that only the dead woods and those with criminal records will be affected." "Dead wood" is never pluralized in BE.

decampees frequently used in Nigeria's political register meaning "to have decamped from one party to another", e.g. "APP aspirant woos decampees back to party." It is derived in analogy with other English forms.

decorate often used to mean "furnish", as in "John's apartment is well-decorated" for BE "John's apartment is tastefully furnished."

dede /dede/ a title of respect which a younger person prefixes to the name of an older person. Thus "Dede Mbakwe"—"my respected elder brother Mbakwe." "Dede" is sometimes used without a name, as in "Dede should they pick before me?" (SL: Igbo).

deep often used for someone who speaks a dialect of a particular language that is typical of the older generation, as in "Chike speaks deep Igbo."

deliver often used transitively in NE in the context of giving birth, as in "She delivered her baby exactly at noon." In BE, "gave birth to" or "was delivered of" would be more appropriate in this circumstance.

demand the preposition "for" is very frequently used in NE after "demand" but not in BE, as in "The workers are demanding for the immediate payment of their leave allowances before calling off the strike."

demobilizer "immobilizer", a device for preventing an automobile from being started, as in "The good demobilizer in my car prevented the thieves from stealing my car after two different attempts."

deportees persons deported from a country, as in "Thirty-two Nigerian deportees were flown into the country last night from Stuttgart, Germany." It is derived in analogy with other English forms.

deprive the collocation "deprive from" is sometimes found in NE where BE speakers would prefer "prevent from", e.g. "I will not deprive you from going to his house, but he will not be welcome in my house." In this sentence, a BE speaker would probably use "prevent you from" rather than "deprive you from." However, the collocation "deprive of" is common in BE usage, as in "It's wrong to suddenly deprive your body of certain foods."

derica cup the smallest unit of measurement for rice, beans and garri.

descend some NE speakers often introduce the particle "down" after "descend" where BE will consider the use of this particle redundant, e.g. "The old man missed his steps and fell as he was descending down the stairs." The particle "down" will not be found in BE in this context since "descend" suggests coming or going down.

develop there is the substitution of "develop" for "get" in the NE idiomatic expression "develop cold feet" which is equivalent to BE "get cold feet", i.e. "to become nervous of doing something, especially something risky or dangerous", e.g. "He developed cold feet at the last minute" for BE "He got cold feet at the last minute."

devotees used in NE to refer to the believers of a particular religious faith. This word which is absent in BE is derived in analogy with other English forms.

diplomatic often used pejoratively in NE where it also means "crafty", e.g. "Nigerian politicians are very diplomatic." In BE, it is never used pejoratively and instead has a complimentary connotation so that "being diplomatic" would mean "being tactful."

discharged in the hospital or prison context, NE speakers often use "to be discharged" where BE speakers use "to be released", e.g. "He was discharged from the hospital yesterday."

discuss about the insertion of a superfluous preposition "about" after this verb is very common in NE. e.g. "We are discussing about the rising cost of marriage in Nigeria." In BE usage, "about" will be considered redundant in this sentence.

disturb sometimes used intransitively, especially at the lower educational level, as in "Stop disturbing" for BE "Stop disturbing me/us"; "Don't disturb" for "Don't disturb me/us." "Disturb" is used transitively in BE.

dobale /dɔbale/ "the act of lying stretched out on the ground as a form of begging or showing remorse." "Dobale" may be equivalent to BE "prostration", e.g. "The most annoying thing is to subject him to that kind of humiliation, to take his video films while he was crying and doing dobale to Abacha." (SL: Yoruba).

dodo /dodo/ fried slices of ripe plantain. (SL: Yoruba).

dogo /dogo/ tall person. (SL: Hausa).

dogoyaro /dogojaro/ particular bitter herb used in the treatment of malaria. (SL: Hausa).

don't mention an ellipsis for "Don't mention it", e.g.
A: Thanks for the food.
B: Don't mention.

don't mind him this is a frequently used NE expression that means "Disregard what he says" or "Don't listen to him."

(don't) take the law into your hands the particle 'own' is omitted in NE idiomatic expression "(Don't) take the law into your hands" which is equivalent to BE "(Don't) take the law into your own hands", i.e. to take no notice of society's rules and act alone, usually by force.

---

door-mouth often used in NE to mean "door-step", as in "Whenever they fail, they put it at the door-mouth of the sports' administrators"; "What he is asking for is just at his door-mouth."

double mind frequently found in NE with the meaning "doubtful", as in "When he introduced the coup plans to me, I told him that I had a double mind about it, but he insisted that it was the decision of the military."

down this particle is often found after some verbs in contexts where it will be considered redundant in BE. Some of these verbs include "bow" (as in bow down), "come" (as in come down), "fall" (as in fall down), "list" (as in list down), "lower" (as in lower down), "pin" (as in pin down), "settle" (as in settle down) and "shoot" (as in shoot down).

down-fall a popularly used saying in Nigeria is "The down-fall of a man is not the end of his life." This saying suggests that one who has fallen today may rise again provided he is alive.

dowry commonly used in NE, meaning "money paid by or on behalf of a man for a woman as his bride." (See bride-price). In BE, "dowry" means "property or money brought by a bride to her husband when they marry."

draw commonly used to mean "to fetch water from the well", as in "Go and draw some water from the well." It is also used in a sitting situation to mean "shift towards me", e.g. "I asked him to draw nearer but he refused."

draw-soup the soup of ogbono or okro which is usually slippery in nature. (See ogbono and okro).

drawers sometimes used to denote pants worn by men. In BE, it refers to knickers or underpants worn by women, especially ones that cover the upper part of the legs.

dress 1. as a verb, it is used in NE to mean "shift one's position." "Please dress for me" can be a request that one should shift one's sitting position to accommodate the person making the request.
2. as a plural noun, it is used to refer either to certain garments worn by men or to certain garments worn by women. BE uses "clothes" in the same sense, but reserves "dresses" as the plural of the noun denoting a one-piece garment worn by women.

dress back commonly used among the less educated NE speakers with the meaning "to move backwards a little." "Please dress back" may be equivalent to BE "Please move backwards."

dress one's bed "to dress one's bed" is an expression commonly used by many Nigerians as an equivalent of BE "to make one's bed", e.g. "She often forgets that she should dress the bed" for BE "She often forgets that she should make the bed."

dress up has the meaning "get dressed", as in "I wonder why it took you two hours to dress up."

drink often used in contexts where it may be equivalent to "take" or "swallow" in reference to tablets or other drugs, as in "Make sure you drink your medicine every morning."

drinking house   "a bar", e.g. "Check me up in the drinking house behind the church."

driver   in Nigeria where there is a tendency to address a person by an occupational title, "Driver" is frequently used as a title for someone who drives a commercial vehicle, as in "Driver, drop me at the next junction." The use of "Driver" as a title is not common in BE.

driver's side   NE users make distinctions between the owner's side, the driver's side and the passenger's side in a motor car. Driver's side is the seat before the steering wheel where the driver has to sit.

drop   sometimes functions intransitively in NE, so that a passenger, for instance, may be heard telling a driver "I will drop at the next junction." "Drop" is not used intransitively in BE. The word "drop" is also sometimes found in the register of letter writing, particularly among the less educated speakers of NE with the meaning "write", as in "I wish to drop you these few lines of letter."

dry   often used derogatorily (especially in descriptions about women) to mean "thin", skinny", as in "She looks very dry."

dry fish   distinction is often made between fresh fish (fish that is frozen) and dry fish (fish that has been dried either in the sun or in the fire), e.g. "Dry fish has suddenly become very costly in the market."

dry season one of the two seasons of the year, beginning from October to April. This season is in contrast to the other season known as "rainy season" beginning from April to September.

dubbing frequently found in the register of examination malpractice, especially among university students meaning "outright copying in the examination hall", e.g. "About four students were caught dubbing in GES 101 examination."

dubious character a frequently heard collocation in NE used to refer to "people suspected to be criminals", e.g. "In a meeting with the leaders of Landlords' Association, the state commissioner of police asked the landlords to always report tenants with dubious character to the police."

duster a piece of cloth or foam used for cleaning the black board that is used for writing in schools. In BE, "duster" means a piece of cloth used for dusting furniture, etc.

E

• **Eaglets** ellipsis for "Golden Eaglets"—the name of Nigeria's under-17 football team.

ear-pain frequently heard in NE for "ear-ache", as in "Please doctor, my ear-pain is getting worse."

ease oneself a polite expression in NE that stands for "going to the toilet", as in "Let me ease myself."

eat 1. frequently used in the register of games such as draughts and chess where BE would use "take", i.e. "to take the opponent's piece", e.g. "Eat first!"
2. often used especially by less educated NE speakers to mean "to extort money from someone", as in "For long, they have been eating my money." "Eat" also collocates with "salt" in NE where BE would probably employ "use", as in "He doesn't eat much salt" for "He doesn't use much salt."
3. the NE idiomatic expression "eat one's cake and have it back" can be said to be an inversion of BE "to have one's cake and eat it", as in "You can't eat your cake and have it back." (See "cake").

eba /eba/ garri prepared with hot water, as in "Please give me eba and egusi soup." (SL: Yoruba).

ECWA acronym for Evangelical Church of West Africa.

---

edikang ikong /edikaŋ ikɔŋ/ popular Efik soup rich in meat, fish and vegetables, as in "Edikang ikong soup." (SL: Efik).

Edo /edo/ an ethnic group in the Edo state of Nigeria. Edo is also the name of the language of the Edo people, and the indigenous name for Benin city—their capital city.

educationally disadvantaged states frequently used to describe states whose citizens embraced western education late. Majority of educationally disadvantaged states are found in the Northern Nigeria because of the early emergence of Islamic education in that part of the country.

ee! an interjection that is equivalent to "do you mean it?" e.g.
A: I heard from BBC this morning that some military officers were arrested for plotting a coup."
B: Ee?
It may also be equivalent to "yes" depending on the tone, e.g.
A: Try to be there very early
B: Ee.
(SL: common to most Nigerian languages).

Efik /efik/ the name for an ethnic group in Cross Rivers and Akwa Ibom states of Nigeria. It is also the name of the language of the Efik people.

efinrin /efiri/ the plant of Ocimum Viride, with a thyme-like odour, whose leaves have a strong fragrant flavour, and can be used in preparing stew. (SL: Yoruba).

Egbe Omo Yoruba /egbe ɔmɔ joruba/ a socio-politico-cultural organization of Yoruba descendants worldwide, as in "Egbe Omo Yoruba has announced the successful debut on Monday May 18, 1998, of a radio program "Voice of Oduduwa." (SL: Yoruba).

egunje /egundʒe/ "bribe", e.g. "Let me tell you, the police men will not allow you to go except you give them egunje." (SL: Yoruba).

egusi /egusi/ melon; melon seeds used for preparing soup, "egusi soup". (Also in WAE, SL: Yoruba).

ehee! an interjection that signifies that the listener understands the story being told, and therefore, encourages the continuation of the story. (SL: common to most Nigerian languages).

eid-il-kabir one of the Muslim festivals widely celebrated in Nigeria, e.g. "The Internal Affairs Minister has declared April 7th as a public holiday in commemoration of Eid-il-kabir festival." (SL: Arabic).

eject this word sometimes collocates with "force" in NE where it will not occur in BE, e.g. "The military government has vowed to forcefully eject ASUU members from university accommodation if they fail to call off the on-going strike by Monday." The use of "forcefully" in this sentence will be considered tautological in BE since "eject" denotes forcing somebody to leave a place.

Eke /eke/ first day of the four-day Igbo week; market that holds on Eke day, as in "Our custom here is that nobody goes to the farm on Eke market day." (SL: Igbo).

eko /ekɔ/ food prepared from maize. It is known as "agidi" among the Igbo. (SL: Yoruba).

ekwe /ekwe/ a wooden musical instrument, hollow inside, as in "Then from the distance came the faint beating of the ekwe." (SL: Igbo).

elderly ellipsis for "an elderly person", it has the same meaning as "an elder" in reference to an older person, as in "Always respect your elders." This means that "an elderly person" may refer to a young adult who is just older than the speaker who may be a child. In BE, "elder" is used comparatively to refer to the older of two closely related members of a family, as in "He is the elder of the two brothers." "Elderly people" in BE refer to people who are rather old (past middle age).

electorate used in NE to mean "voters in an election", as in "All the electorate should participate in the voters' revision exercise scheduled for next week." In BE, "electorate" refers to "all the electors considered as a group", e.g. "The opposition leader was favoured by the majority of the electorate."

elubo /elubɔ/ yam or cassava flour. (SL: Yoruba).

ember months the months from September to December are frequently referred to as ember months in Nigeria, and are believed to be dangerous months, when people are more prone to accidents, e.g. "The

Federal Road Safety Corps (FRSC) have advised drivers to drive carefully during these ember months."

emir /emia/ king or ruler, e.g. "The Emir of Kano." (SL: Arabic).

emphasize many speakers of NE use the preposition "on" redundantly after "emphasize" in NE , e.g. "The Chairman emphasized on the need for members to pay their annual dues promptly." The use of the preposition "on" after "emphasize" in BE would be considered redundant, e.g. "He emphasized the importance of careful driving."

EMU an acronym for Eastern Mandate Union, a socio-political organization for the nine eastern states.

ending used in NE in expressions of time after the name of a month, e.g. "Your arrears of salary will be paid in full by March ending." In BE, it would be "...by the end of March."

engage in discussions about marriage, it is used in NE in a way different from BE, e.g. "Segun has engaged Chika." This NE expression will be expressed in BE as "Segun and Chika have got engaged."

engagement ceremony this is a pre-wedding ceremony or marriage ceremony common among the Yoruba in which the traditional rites of marriage are observed. It is known as "traditional marriage" in other parts of Nigeria. "Engagement ceremony" usually precedes the church wedding.

English medicine this collocation refers to foreign or orthodox medicine as opposed to traditional medicine, e.g. "English medicine is no longer effective for the treatment of malaria."

enjoy this verb is more frequently used as a transitive verb in BE. In NE, it regularly occurs intransitively, e.g. "Bola has been enjoying since her husband went to the US." In BE, this sentence would take a direct object so that the above sentence will become "Bola has been enjoying herself since her husband went to the US."

enter in NE, "enter" is frequently heard for "come in", e.g. "Enter and close the door because of mosquitoes." In BE, "enter" is used in very formal contexts such as "to enter into an agreement" or "to enter a building." A more appropriate BE version of the sentence would be "Come in and close the door because of mosquitoes."

enter with change frequently shouted by bus conductors and taxi drivers as a warning that commuters should have their actual fare on them, e.g. "Enter with your change. No five five naira" for BE "Ensure that you have your actual fare on you. I do not have change."

entertain fears a collocation used in both formal and informal styles in NE, meaning "be afraid", e.g. "She is entertaining some fears that her husband's second wife may poison her." In BE, "entertain fears" is considered appropriate only in formal style.

environmental ellipsis for "environmental sanitation

day", the one day each month when law-abiding people must spend the morning hours cleaning up the environment, e.g. "We must not go out before 10 a.m. because today is environmental." "Environmental day" is also found in NE for "environmental sanitation day", e.g. "Don't forget that tomorrow is environmental day."

enyi /eɲi/ "friend", commonly used by the Igbo. It can also be used to address one who is not really a friend in order to attract his attention, as in "Enyi, let me ask you." (SL: Igbo).

equipment this noun is used as a non-count in BE. NE speakers have a tendency to use the plural form, as in "The Sports minister has ordered for more equipments for the completion of Abuja central stadium." (Also in WAE).

escort used frequently in NE to also mean "accompany" or "see off someone" who may be a regular visitor to the house. It is part of Nigerian culture to accompany guests to some distance before turning back. So, "let me escort you" is often suggested by the host, when his visitor is about to leave. In BE, "escort" is primarily used in the sense of police or military protection.

essential commodities government agencies often purchase certain commodities such as salt, vegetable oil, rice, milk, etc. and sell them to their staff at subsidized prices. Such commodities as listed here are usually referred to as "essential commodities."

esusu /esusu/ savings club. (SL: Yoruba).

European often used to refer to any white man, including Americans, Australians, Chinese, etc.

evening NE speakers often use the greeting "Good evening" as from 4 p.m., much earlier than the speakers of BE. In Britain, evening begins at 5 p.m., i.e. at the end of the working day.

everytime always, most times, as in "She dresses well everytime."

evict the adverb "forcefully" sometimes collocates with "evict" in contexts where it will not be found in BE, e.g. "A middle-aged man and his wife who were forcefully evicted from their house eight years ago by Brig. Raji Rasaki have dragged Lagos state government to court over the violation of their housing rights." "Force" or "forcefully" may not collocate with "evict" in BE usage since "evict" denotes the removal of somebody from a house or land with the support of the law.

evidence this noun is rarely pluralized in BE, but very frequently pluralized in NE, e.g. "The government has several evidences to prove that the military officers who are being detained were actually planning a coup which would have left the Head of State and many senior government officials dead."

ewedu /ewedu/ soup prepared with "ewedu vegetable", as in "ewedu soup". (SL: Yoruba).

ewo! /ewo/ exclamation expressing surprise, and may be equivalent to "Oh!" (SL: Igbo).

exchange ideas a regularly heard NE collocation, especially within educational institutions, is "to exchange ideas" which may be equivalent to BE "to have conversation", "to have discussion, "to share ideas", e.g. "There has to be a forum to exchange ideas" for BE "There has to be a forum to have discussion." In BE, "exchange" can collocate with "blows", "glances", greetings", but not with "ideas".

excursion frequently used among students in educational institutions to represent the sense of BE "outing", as in "The student-members of the Alpha club went on an excursion to Port Harcourt." In BE, "excursion" means "a short journey, especially one made by a group of people together for pleasure", e.g. "Your tour includes a one-day excursion to the Grand Canyon by air."

expect also used to mean "to be pregnant", as in "My wife is expecting a child very soon" for BE "My wife is expected to give birth to a child soon."

expensive joke commonly used as a slang among students to mean an unacceptable joke which might bring some regret to the person making the joke, e.g. "Any junior student who thinks he can crack expensive jokes with the senior prefect will be severely punished."

expired often used rather derogatorily to mean "late" or "dead", as in "The expired head of state" for "The late head of state."

explain the reason 'explain' and 'the reasons' often

collocate in NE but not in BE, e.g. "Explain the reason why I should go" for BE "Give the reason why I should go" or "Explain why I should go."

expo a clipped form for "exposition", referring to the leakage of examination question, as in "Their results were seized because they were involved in expo."

extended family a family structure common in Nigeria where many individuals trace their descent from a common ancestor, house, or lineage. As a result, they see themselves as constituting a unit that imposes obligations of mutual assistance on all of them. A "family" in Britain consists of a husband, wife and their children. (Also in WAE).

eye fraternity /eje frɘtɜ:niti/ a secret cult popular among university students.

eyeing "to be eyeing someone" is a NE idiomatic expression meaning " pay special attention to a girl in whom one is interested", as in "I have been eyeing that girl from the first day I met her."

eye-service idiomatically used to mean "to pretend to be nice to one's boss in order to derive some favour", e.g. "I hate eye-service." Eye-service may also refer to an unfaithful employee, as in "She does eye-service a lot" for BE "She is a very unfaithful employee."

Eyo masquerade /ejɔ mæskuredi/ masquerade festival that is celebrated annually in Lagos.

Eze /eze/ "king" or traditional ruler. (SL: Igbo).

F

face is scarce a commonly heard expression in NE is "Your face is scarce nowadays" for BE "One hardly comes across you nowadays."

face-me-I-face-you a building style (usually inhabited by people of low income group) in which rooms face one another along a narrow streak known as passage or corridor in a bungalow or storey building, as in "Dear reader, do you or someone you know live in a face-me-I-face-you house?"

fact the plural form of this noun is sometimes found in NE, e.g. "The report of the panel was based on facts." In BE, this noun is normally singular.

fail woefully a NE collocation commonly used within educational institutions to describe performances in examinations. For instance, when a lecturer tells his students, "Many of you failed woefully in my course", he may be implying that many students performed badly in his course or that he is simply not satisfied with their performance.

fair in educational context, "fair" in BE means "average", "quite good". In Nigeria's educational context, "fair" has no definite meaning so that, depending on the user, it may mean "very good", "not good", "average", etc.

fall this verb is often followed by "down" in NE, e.g. "The value of Naira is still falling down despite the fiscal measures outlined in this year's budget." The adverbial particle "down" would be considered redundant in BE.

fall victim of "of" often substitutes for "to" in the NE idiomatic usage "fall victim of" which is equivalent to BE "fall victim to", meaning "to be hurt, killed, damaged or destroyed by something", e.g. "The former minister fell victim of armed robbery attack" for BE "The former minister fell victim to armed robbery attack."

false witness often heard where BE would prefer "false evidence", as in "You gave false witness" for BE "You gave false evidence."

fancy "decoration", as in:
A: For you to have the posters of General Sani Abacha in your sitting-room means you like his government.
B: No, they are just for fancy.

far frequently used in NE to indicate distance, e.g. "I live far (away) from the university." In BE, this construction would likely be "I live a long way (away) from the university." When the NE sentence is found in BE, it is used to stress the seriousness of the distance.

fast "fast" is substituted for "quick" in the NE idiomatic expression "as fast as lightening" which is equivalent to BE "as quick as lightening", meaning "very quickly".

fast-fast a reduplicative frequently used in NE with the meaning "as quickly as possible", e.g. "Please get me two more bottles of beer fast-fast."

fatal accident very serious accident, as in, "The fatal accident left him paralyzed."

father the person addressed as "father" may be one's uncle or an elder in one's village. The same applies to "mother".

fault this word is often found in the plural form in NE, e.g. "Why are you always finding faults with your friends?" This noun is never used in the plural form with -s in BE.

FCT an abbreviation for Federal Capital Territory, which is located in Abuja.

FEAP an acronym for Family Economic Advancement Programme—a pet project of the First Lady under General Abdulsalami Abubakar's administration. It was primarily aimed at enhancing the living standard of women.

FEC an acronym for Federal Executive Council, i.e. members of the executive arm of government at the federal level, as in "The decision was taken yesterday at the federal executive council meeting, presided over by the President."

FEDECO an acronym for Federal Electoral

Commission, which conducted elections in 1979 and 1983.

federal character the concept of drawing from a broad range of constituencies is affectionately known as "federal character" in Nigeria. It is a policy of the federal government of Nigeria in which admissions to educational institutions and appointments to positions in federal establishments reflect the regional divisions of the country.

fellow in BE, it refers to someone of the male sex. In NE, it is extended to include a female, and also a "colleague", e.g. "She is a fellow student"; "She is a fellow colleague"; "He is a fellow teacher."

fetch a frequently used collocation in NE is "to fetch water" which may mean "to carry/bring water" in BE, e.g. "Have you fetched some water from the well?"

few lines of mine sometimes heard in NE in the context of letter writing where BE would use "letter", as in "I am glad to write you these few lines of mine" for BE "I am glad to write this letter to you."

fidau the eighth day Moslem prayer for a dead person, e.g. "All markets in Lagos will be shut on Saturday to mark the eighth day Moslem fidau prayer for the late Nigerian politician Moshood Abiola." (SL: Arabic).

find fault frequently used in NE meaning "ready to pick out little faults", as in "He is always finding faults with everybody in his department."

---

find trouble often heard, particularly at the lower educational level to mean being troublesome, e.g. "Every member of staff likes Mr. Oke because he doesn't find trouble" for BE "Every member of staff likes Mr. Oke because he is not troublesome."

fine-fine a reduplicative meaning "several fine", e.g. "I visited my friend's campus and I saw many fine-fine girls with fine-fine legs."

finish this verb is more frequently used intransitively in NE than in BE, e.g. in the context of buying and selling, as in:
A: I want to buy a tin of peak milk.
B: It has finished.
"It has finished" would be represented in BE as "It has been sold out." Other examples include: "His money is finished"; "Have you finished?" and "My biro is finished."

fire! the shout of "Fire!" is often heard in a gathering where the speaker is criticizing people in positions of authority, as a way of encouraging him to keep on "firing". In this context, "fire" means "criticize", "rebuke" or "scold". Apart from its other uses, this verb may be used in BE in informal style with the meaning "to dismiss an employee from a job", as in "She was fired for mismanagement of fund."

first-born the eldest child in a family, as in "My first-born is now in the university."

fisi /fisi/ discount usually in the form of additional

quantity, as in "Customer, fisi", meaning "Customer, add some quantity free of charge." (SL: Yoruba).

fit "fit" is substituted for "fill" in the NE idiomatic expression "fit into somebody's shoes" which is equivalent to BE "fill somebody's shoes", meaning "to take over somebody's function, duties, etc. and perform them in a satisfactory way", e.g. "It will be difficult for anybody to fit into the late Oba's shoes" for "It will be difficult for anybody to fill the late Oba's shoes."

fito /fito/ alcoholic drink brewed from guinea-corn. (SL: Hausa).

flit "to spray", as in "You should always flit your room before you sleep to avoid mosquito bite." In BE, this would probably be "You should always spray your room with insecticide before you sleep to avoid mosquito bite."

flying boat speed boat.

Flying Eagles the name of Nigeria's under-21 football team.

flying colours brilliant performance, as in "I am working hard so that I can pass my school certificate examinations in flying colours."

follow has an extended meaning that includes "accompany" or "go with", as in "Can I follow you to Jide's house?", meaning "Can I accompany you to Jide's house?"; "Follow me" for "Come along." In BE, this verb is used with the meaning "(to cause something) to come, go or take place after somebody/something else in space, time or order", e.g. "His dog follows him everywhere"; "Friday follows Thursday"; "The lightening was quickly followed by heavy thunder." Also, the preposition "in" is omitted in the NE idiomatic usage "follow somebody's footsteps" which is equivalent to BE "follow in somebody's footsteps", i.e. "to do as somebody else does", e.g. "He follows his father's footsteps in working as a lawyer." In BE version of this idiom, there must be the preposition "in".

followership frequently used in BE with the meaning "following", as in "The pastor's style of preaching has attracted a large followership to the church" for BE "The pastor's style of preaching has attracted a large following to the church."

food   in NE, "food" excludes meat, vegetable, fruits, biscuits, snacks, etc. It denotes staple food such as rice, yam, garri, amala, foo-foo, beans, etc. "Food" in BE includes all the items listed above.

foo-foo /fuːfuː/ food prepared from cassava and eaten in balls with soup. It is sometimes spelt as 'fufu'. Among the Igbo, it is known as "akpu". (Also in WAE, SL: Yoruba).

for in NE, this preposition substitutes for "by" in the context of marriage and childbearing, as in "My wife already has three children for me." This will be expressed in BE as "My wife already has three children by me."

force "the force" is often used in NE to denote the

"Army", as in "My ambition is to join the force." In BE, "the force" is often used to refer to the Police, while the plural, "the Forces", is used to refer to the Armed Forces.

foreign "imported goods", as in "There is no locally-made shoe here. They are all foreign."

forget commonly found in NE with the meaning "leave something behind", as in "I forgot my bunch of keys in John's house" for BE "I left my bunch of keys in John's house." In BE, this verb is normally found with the meaning "to fail to remember or recall something", and so will not be used in phrases indicating static location as complement. It will be found in such BE examples as "I forgot his birthday"; "She probably forgot that I will be coming."

four-one-nine "a dupe", as in "Two four-one-nine suspects were yesterday arraigned before Ikeja magistrate court for trying to dupe an Italian businessman of $2m." It is also found in BE as a past tense verb meaning "duped", as in "These unlucky ones toil for the semi-literate or literate traders for years on end, tidying things up for them only to be 419ed or receive toad for supper at the end of it all."

frankly speaking frankly, speaking honestly, e.g. "Frankly speaking, you have failed" for BE "Frankly, you have failed" or "Speaking honestly, you have failed."

FRCN an abbreviation for Federal Radio Corporation of Nigeria.

free of charge completely free, as in "She gave me a room for two years free of charge."

freedom "doing one's freedom" may be used in the context of apprentices, who at the end of their apprenticeship, often mark the occasion of their discharge by their masters with a party, e.g. "Toyin is doing her freedom this evening and I must be there."

fresh-fish fish sold "fresh" and different from dried fish or smoked fish.

freshers frequently found in the register of higher educational institutions referring to new students, as in "The Chapel of the Resurrection, University of Ibadan, Ibadan, Nigeria, heartily welcomes all students, freshers and stalites alike to the University of Ibadan."

fried egg in Britain, to fry an egg, one does not need to mix the yoke and the white before or during frying. But in Nigeria, "fried egg" means that the yoke and the white together with other ingredients are mixed before frying, thereby producing BE equivalent of "scrambled egg" or "omelette".

fried rice "fried rice" in Nigeria is similar to "jollof rice". The difference lies in the preparation. Jollof rice is prepared with all the required ingredients added while cooking is still on, fried rice is prepared simply by mixing the fried stew or sauce with the cooked rice.

from speakers of NE often use the preposition "from" in contexts where BE usage will prefer "on", e.g. "Activities marking Nigeria's 38 years of independence will start from Sunday, September 27 with prayer in churches throughout the country." BE will use "on" instead of "from".

from the foregoing many users of NE say "From the foregoing" when they mean "In conclusion", as in "From the foregoing, I have no doubt in my mind that the centralization of the army is a design by the North to permanently hold on to power in the country." In BE, "foregoing" denotes "preceding" or "just mentioned."

from the onset "onset" sometimes replaces "outset" in the NE expression "From the on-set" which is equivalent to BE "From the out-set", i.e. from the beginning, e.g. "From the on-set, you got things wrong" for BE "From the out-set, you got things wrong."

from the scratch "the" is added in the NE idiomatic expression "From the scratch" which is equivalent to BE "From scratch", i.e. starting from zero or with nothing. E.g. "He started from the scratch" for BE "He started from scratch."

from the word go from the beginning, as in "From the word go, you are the cause of this problem" for BE "From the beginning, you have been the cause of this problem."

frown often used transitively in NE, as in "She suddenly frowned her face when she realized that the man was not going to give her some money." In BE, "her face" would be redundant.

FRSC an abbreviation for Federal Road Safety Commission, e.g. "He is the longest serving senior management staff of the FRSC."

fruit 1. this noun is often pluralized in the NE idiomatic usage "bear some fruits" which is equivalent to BE "bear fruit", i.e. "to have or bring about a result, usually a successful one", e.g. "With reference to the chapel hall project, I am happy to announce that our prayer and efforts have started bearing some fruits." The noun "fruit" is not normally found in the plural form in the BE version of this idiomatic expression. Apart from the idiomatic usage, this noun is also pluralized in NE contexts where it is not in BE, e.g. "We need to buy fruits and vegetables" for BE "We need to buy fruit and vegetables."
2. it is also the name for a fruit with thin fleshy fibroid surface and hard shell within which lies an edible nut.

FSP an abbreviation for Family Support Programme, a pet project of the First Lady under General Abacha's regime.

fuel this is equivalent to "petrol" in BE.

Fuji (music) /fudʒi/ it originated from the Muslim Ramadan festival as music usually employed to wake up Muslims during their festival. It is today often perceived as a brand of music played primarily by Muslim musicians.

Fulani /fʊlani/ one of the major ethnic groups in the northern Nigeria, famous for cattle rearing.

full current also known as high current, it is frequently used in NE where BE would use "full voltage", as in "We always have full current in our area."

full the bucket fill the bucket, commonly used by less educated NE speakers, as in "please full my bucket" for BE "Please fill my bucket with water."

fura /fura/ often known as local yoghurt, it is a liquid concoction made from millet-flour, spices, sour milk, sugar, etc. mostly consumed at lunch time, e.g. "Milk is often consumed at lunch time as fura danono." (SL: Hausa).

furniture often pluralized in NE, as in "He has good furnitures in his sitting-room." This word is rarely pluralized in BE. (Also in WAE).

further-studies 1. as an adjective, it means "higher education", e.g. "Boma will be going to the University of Ibadan for further-studies."
2. as a verb, "to further one's studies/education" is often found in informal contexts in NE where BE would prefer "to study", e.g. "I will be going to the University of Lagos to further my education." The more likely expression in BE would be "I will be going to the University of Lagos to study." The expression "to further one's studies" is found only in very formal contexts in BE.

future-husband commonly used by the less educated speakers of NE to mean "fiancé" or "fiancée", e.g. "My daughter's future-husband is still a student" for BE "My daughter's fiancé is still a student."

G

G-34 frequently used in NE to refer to a pan-Nigerian group of eminent conservatives, progressives and radicals led by Alex Ekwueme, former vice-president, which sent a powerful memorandum to General Abacha, in which it raised objections to his consensus candidacy on moral, legal, and constitutional grounds, as in "The G-34 also condemned the amendments of the constitution for the adoption of Abacha as illegal."

gala /gala/ a kind of snacks usually sold mainly to motorists and other travelers along the road.

gallon commonly used in NE to also mean "container", usually made of metal, as in "Did you bring any gallon?", meaning "Did you bring any container?" In BE, a "gallon" is a unit of measurement for liquids, equal to about 4.5 litres.

gallop this is used as a noun in NE to mean "pothole" in a bad road, and may have been derived from the movement characteristic of the galloping of a horse, e.g. "Drivers avoid plying that road because of gallops."

gangan /gɔgɔ/ traditional drum. (SL: Yoruba).

garage also used in NE in the sense of "motor park", i.e. a terminus where all kinds of vehicles are boarded, as in "I am going to the garage to board a vehicle to Onitsha." In BE, "garage" refers to "a place where vehicles are repaired and sold and where petrol and oil may also be bought."

garden in NE, "garden" seems to be devoted only for vegetables. In BE, "garden" is "a piece of private ground used for growing flowers, fruit, vegetables, etc., typically with a lawn or other open space for playing or relaxing."

garden-egg also known as eggplant (of Solanum melongena); a round, white or green-coloured fruit often used for the entertainment of guests. Its leaves are used as vegetable.

garden city a euphemistic name for Port Harcourt, given because of the beauty of the city.

garri/gari /gari/ cassava flour; cassava tubers grated and fried to semi-coarse flour; fried grated cassava flour which is eaten in a variety of ways. It is processed by drying, grinding, filtering and frying, e.g. "Garri that used to be a poor man's food is today out of the reach of the common man." Distinctions are often made between "red garri" (i.e. garri fried with some red oil) and "white garri", as in "While a bag of red garri is sold for N850.00, the white type is sold for N800.00." (Also in WAE, SL: Yoruba / Hausa).

gate-man commonly used in NE for "gate-keeper", as in "ASUU has described as unacceptable a situation where gate-men in the Central Bank of Nigeria earn more than university professors."

gate-fee commonly used in NE for "admission fee", as in "Only those who pay their gate-fee will be allowed to enter the hall." (Also in WAE).

GCFR Grand Commander of the Order of the Federal Republic—the highest Nigerian national honour, usually awarded to former and serving heads of state.

GCON Grand Commander of the Order of the Niger— Nigeria's second highest national honour, usually awarded to former and serving Vice Presidents and other such persons of very high achievements.

gele /gele/ women's headgear. (SL: Yoruba).

gentle widely used in NE to describe a person who is well-behaved, quiet, decently dressed, respectful and unassuming. Although it may be related slightly to its meanings in BE, however, "gentle" in BE is commonly used to describe a behaviour that is kind, mild, careful, not rough or violent, as in "I prefer lux to most other soaps because it is gentle to the skin." In NE, "gentle" is very frequently used to describe human beings, as in "gentleman", "gentlewoman", "gentleboy", etc.

gentleman's grade frequently used in the context of university degree results to describe second class lower division, which is attained by students who are neither too intelligent nor too weak, e.g.
A: What class of degree did you make?
B: Just a gentleman's grade.

george a two-piece cloth material tied around the waist by women, especially in the Eastern Nigeria. It is made of cotton, or sometimes silk material, often patterned with brightly coloured checks, e.g. "All this topped the kind of george material that had never before been seen in Ibuza."

german-mango a kind of mango that looks very greenish outwardly while it is already ripe.

get NE speakers often use "get" interchangeably with "make", "go", or "become", as in "We got much money from that job" for BE "We made much money from that job"; "Letters get missing in Nigeria's post offices very often" for BE "Letters go missing in Nigeria's post offices very often"; "Don't exchange words with him any longer. Otherwise, the situation will get bad" for BE "Don't exchange words with him any longer. Otherwise, the situation will go bad"; "The topic will get clear to you at the end of the lecture" for "The topic will become clear to you at the end of the lecture". Also, "get" is sometimes used in NE in situations where its use is unnecessary, e.g. "Go and get those shoes polished" for BE "Go and polish those shoes." Get is also frequently found in the register of students, where it refers to scores or marks, e.g. "What did you get in that course?" for BE "What did you score in that course?"

get down the expression, "get down" is very frequently used in NE with reference to leaving a vehicle where BE would prefer "get out", as in "Let me get down here." A BE user would likely say "Let me get out here." The use of "get out" in NE denotes rudeness or harshness.

Ghana-must-go a hard bag for carrying large quantity

of goods. The bag is believed to be made in Ghana or by Ghanaians in Nigeria, e.g. "When the customs saw the palm oil in my Ghana-must-go bag, they insisted that I must give them N300.00 or leave the oil behind." It is sometimes also used metaphorically to denote money—a reference to the use of the sack to carry money, as in "Seventy-four of my colleagues backing me cannot be bribed. And no volume of Ghana-must-go bag can save the situation."

ghostworkers a phrase frequently used in Nigeria to describe dead, sacked, retired or non-existent workers whose salaries are still collected by unknown persons, as in "Nearly 4000 ghost workers have been discovered on the pay roll of Niger state government."

ginkana /dʒinkana/ locally-brewed gin popular in Rivers and Bayelsa states.

girl often used in NE to denote a female servant or apprentice of whatever age, as in "She is my girl and not my sister."

girlfriend a female friend with whom one sleeps. This is equivalent to BE "lover."

give this verb collocates differently from BE in a number of ways. Consider, for instance:
1. "A well-known professor from Britain will give a keynote address at the conference." BE speakers usually "deliver" a key-note address or speech.
2. "The lecturer gave me 40% in his course" instead of "The lecturer scored me 40% in his course" which will

be more likely in BE usage.

give chance often used especially to subordinates or younger people for BE "Excuse me" or "Could you let me pass?" "Give chance" or "give way" may be considered rude if used to a superior or an older person.

give me your ears commonly heard in NE for BE "Lend me your years."

give up a clipped form of BE idiomatic expression "give up the ghost", meaning "die". "The old man finally gave up this morning" would be understood in NE to be that "The old man finally died this morning."

globe often used in NE for "electric bulb".

go the use of "gone" and "been" as two forms of the past participle of this verb often leads to the use of "gone" in NE in contexts where BE would use "been", e.g. "I have not gone to Benin this year"; "Have you ever gone to London?"; "I have not gone home since this semester." In BE, "gone" denotes departure and implies that the person who has departed has not returned, e.g. "Has Peter gone home yet?" On the other hand, "been", usually with an adverb or a prepositional phrase indicating destination, is used to indicate that the person has been to some place and returned, e.g. "I have been abroad many times"; "My friend has never been to Texas." In the three NE examples cited above, BE would prefer "been" to "gone". In another sense, NE speakers often have the tendency to use the preposition "for" redundantly after the verb "go", as in

"She will go for shopping in the evening" for BE "She will go shopping this evening."

go a-borrowing the use of "go a-borrowing" would today sound archaic in BE where "go borrowing" or "go about borrowing" will be preferred. In NE, it is sometimes heard in both formal and informal contexts, e.g. "For us to be able to complete our electricity project this year, we won't have any option other than to go a-borrowing."

go on in the register of public transportation, "go on" is frequently used by bus conductors as a signal to drivers that they are free to continue going having off-loaded or collected passengers on the way. In big cities, it is used as a way of asking drivers not to stop at a particular bus stop because nobody has indicated any interest to stop, as in when a conductor shouts, "Obanikoro! Go on." London bus conductors say "Carry on!" for the same signal.

go on exile the preposition "on" sometimes substitutes for "into" in the NE expression "go on exile" which is equivalent to BE "go into exile", as in "During his regime, many prominent Nigerians were forced to go on exile." In BE, "on" will be replaced by "into" in this sentence.

go-slow commonly used in BE for "traffic-jam", "hold-up", e.g. "In Lagos, we leave for work very early to avoid go-slow." In BE, the expression "go slow" is used in the context of workers deciding to work slowly, especially as a protest or to make their employer meet their demands.

go straight   "on" is frequently omitted in the NE expression "go straight" which is equivalent to BE "go straight on", i.e. an instruction often given to someone as a way of directing him not to turn left or right from the straight road. In BE, "go straight" is an idiomatic expression which means "to live an honest life after being a criminal", as in "It is hoped that the pardoned criminals will come out of prison and go straight."

goat-head   a delicacy prepared using the head of a goat and mixing it with other ingredients. It is also known as "isi-ewu".

godfather   also refers to a person in a position to grant a favour to someone usually related to him, e.g. "I am not afraid of unemployment because I have a god-father", meaning "I am not afraid of unemployment because I have a person who can use his influence or connection to get me a job." In BE, "god-father" is primarily used to refer to "a male godparent", i.e. "a male sponsor at baptism." (Also in WAE).

Godfatherism   the practice of employing or promoting persons not by merit but through personal relationship, or by favour.

goodluck   formed in agglutination for BE 'good luck'.

good day   NE greeting in the afternoon, but unlike BE "good afternoon" which starts from noon to about 5 p.m., "good day" could be heard much earlier and much later.

good enough "good enough" functions in BE only as an adjectival phrase in the complement position, as in "Your effort wasn't good enough." In addition to this function, "good enough" is often used by some NE speakers as a sentence initial adverb equivalent to BE "fortunately", e.g. "Buglers broke into my house yesterday. Good enough there wasn't much for them to steal."

got an accident had an accident, as in "He got an accident" for Be "He had an accident."

Government House the official residence of the Governor of a state.

government work civil service or public service, as in "My wife is doing government work" for BE "My wife is in civil service"; "My wife is a government worker" for BE "My wife is a civil servant."

graduate an ellipsis for "a university graduate", e.g. "Her first son is a graduate."

gragra /gragra/ actions aimed at being noticed or to create fear in some people, as in "You don't just sit and wait for somebody to donate an office to you. You have to begin to make gragra"; it also means to be unduly quarrelsome, as in "Why are you always making gragra?" (SL: Pidgin).

grammar often used to also mean high-sounding English often aimed at impressing the audience, as in "I don't have time for grammar this morning." In BE, "grammar" may refer to the rules of using a language or to a person's knowledge and use of a language, as in "The principles of English grammar"; "He's trying to improve his grammar."

grass among the smokers of marijuana, the term "grass" is commonly used to mean "marijuana", e.g. "Do you take grass?" for "Do you smoke marijuana?"

green a type of vegetable usually very greenish, used for making soup, stew and yam porridge.

green revolution a phrase that came into NE from the late 1970s as part of federal military government's policy to boost food production, e.g. "It was reliably gathered that the new grain crop is part of an anticipated global green revolution to raise productivity of important staple foods so as to meet world's food needs."

guava a tough-limbed tree bearing one of many varieties of roundish, yellow-skinned fruit, sweet or sour, in which many hard tiny seeds are embedded.

guerrilla journalism this collocation is frequently heard in Nigeria, especially under repressive military regimes to describe the practice of journalism in which the contact addresses of the journalists and their news magazines are not known. Usually, these news magazines are anti-military and so have to keep their operations secret. Magazines popularly associated with "guerilla journalism" are *Tell*, *Tempo*, and *The News*.

guguru /guguru/ dried corn fried and eaten as food.

guinea brocade commonly used in NE for clothing

material used in making traditional wears, as in "He was dressed in a deep blue guinea brocade babariga attire."

guy In BE, "guy" is most frequently used to mean "man" or "fellow", but in NE, this meaning is extended to include "an outgoing, self-assured young man", i.e. a person who behaves in a manner to impress others by his striking way of dressing, manner of speech, walking, etc. e.g. "All these students making guy always perform badly in the examination." To "behave like a guy" in NE usage would mean to behave impressively.

gwongworo /gwongworo/ term for any big lorry. (SL: Igbo).

H

haba /haba/ an interjection that expresses disapproval. It may be equivalent to "Don't say that!" or "God forbid!", as in "Last week, he propagated the view that the legislator escaped assassination because of his opposition to the governor. Haba! Is this the kind of utterance expected from an elder statesman?" (SL: Hausa).

had it been that sometimes found in BE as a conditional clause, but more commonly used in NE, especially at the lower educational level as an equivalent of "If + pronoun + had", e.g. "Had it been that you listened to my advice, you would have saved your money" for BE "If you had listened to my advice, you would have saved your money."

hail from in NE, this is used in the sense of "come from" to refer to one's birth place or "home-town". The NE question, "Where do you hail from?" would sound old-fashioned in BE which would prefer "Where do you come from."

hajia /hadʒia/ title for a Muslim woman who has been to Mecca on holy pilgrimage. This is also known as "alhaja". (SL: Arabic).

---

hajj pilgrimage to Mecca made by Muslims, as in "The minister has received several petitions in connection with the manner in which this year's hajj was handled." (SL: Arabic).

half-bag a unit of measurement for rice, beans, garri, sugar, etc. equivalent to about a hundred weight, as in "Only last month, I bought half-bag of rice and half-bag of garri for them, but now everything is already finished."

half-caste referring to people of mixed blood, as in "John is a half-caste: His mother is a Nigerian while his father is a Swede." NE also uses "half-blood" to mean the same thing as "half-caste."

half current also known as "low current", it is frequently used where the BE would use "low voltage", i.e. electricity that is not full to capacity, e.g. "There is electricity right now, but it is half current."

half dozen in NE, "half dozen" is heard instead of BE "half a dozen" and the preposition "of" is redundantly used after "half dozen", e.g. "I want half dozen of eggs" for BE "I want half a dozen eggs."

half-half a reduplicative, frequently used colloquially in NE where BE would prefer "half each", e.g. "Give me half-half bag of rice and beans" for BE "Give me half bag each of rice and beans."

hand "hand" is often added in the NE idiomatic usage "give somebody's hand in marriage (to somebody)" which is equivalent to BE "give somebody in marriage (to somebody)", i.e. "to give the care of one's daughter to her new husband", e.g. "The bride's hand was given in marriage to Oluwole by Chief Johnson, on behalf of the bride's late father."

handbag any bag with a handle, including brief-case, wallet, etc., carried by both men and women, as in "I plan to buy a small handbag for my lectures when next I have some money"; "He rummaged through my handbag containing only my wears and books." In BE, "handbag" is equivalent to American English "purse", i.e. "a small bag for money, keys, etc, carried especially by women."

hand-work refers to a profession which one has learnt after a period of apprenticeship. Professions, which are recognized as handwork in Nigeria, include tailoring, mechanic, plumbing, shoemaking, barbing, driving, brick-laying. They are so-called because, originally, such jobs are manually done. "He has a good hand-work" would mean that he is practising one of the above-mentioned professions, which are lucrative.

harlot this word sounds archaic in BE and may only feature in colloquial style while "prostitute" features in formal style. In NE, both "harlot" and "prostitute" are used in both formal and informal styles. However, it appears a distinction is sometimes made between the two words based on character. While a "harlot" is seen to be living in a brothel, a "prostitute" may simply stand by the roadside or visit clubs in search of men. The second distinction often observed is based on the level of education of NE users. While less educated users frequently use "harlot", the educated speakers prefer "prostitute" with the same meaning.

harmattan one of the seasons in Nigeria; associated with cold weather and dusty wind blowing southwards from the Sahara, usually in December and January, as in "It was a fairly chilly night, for the season of the harmattan wind was fast approaching."

has/have often used to mean own/owns, as in "Who has this key? for BE "Who owns this key?"

Hausa /hausa/ one of the three major ethnic groups in Nigeria, as in "Hausa people." It is also the name of the language spoken by the Hausa people, one of the three indigenous official languages widely used in northern Nigeria.

have 1. frequently used in NE to mean "own", as in "Vita now has a car" for BE "Vita now owns a car."
2. often used in BE where NE would prefer "hold", as in "I have an M.A. degree in History" for BE "I hold an MA degree in History."
3. many NE speakers use "have" for BE "suffer from", as in "He has fever" for BE "He suffers from fever."

head is full of book often used colloquially to mean "knowledgeable", "intelligent", as in "Boma's head is full of book" for BE "Boma is very knowledgeable."

headmaster in Nigeria, "headmaster" or "headmistress" is reserved for the head of a primary school only. In BE, it can refer to the head of a primary

---

or secondary school.

head-tie commonly used in NE for "scarf" or "head-gear", e.g. "Then they would add the type of heavy head-tie that went with native lappas."

hear 1. often used in NE to mean "understand" a language, as in "I don't hear Yoruba" for BE "I don't understand Yoruba."
2. many NE speakers use "hear" for BE "perceive" so that the question "Do you hear the smell of a dead rat?" would be equivalent to BE "DO you perceive the smell of a dead rat?"
3. it may also be used where BE uses "listen to", as in "Are you hearing him?"

heavy frequently used to also mean "to be pregnant", as in "She is heavy" meaning that she is pregnant.

hei! exclamation that expresses surprise. (SL: common to most southern languages).

help often used redundantly in NE expressions. For instance, the NE request, "Please help me call Bode" would be equivalent to BE "Please call Bode for me." The sentence, "Please help me call Bode" would imply that two persons (the speaker and the addressee) are involved in the act of calling Bode.

herbal medicine the art of healing the sick or sickness using the preventive and curative properties of herbs, as in "Herbal medicine is the best cure for kidney problems."

---

herbalist a herbalist is a traditional medicine-man who specializes in the sale and use of herbs for healing purposes. In Nigeria, a "herbalist" is believed to possess some supernatural power so that the same person can be consulted as a diviner or fortune-teller. (Also in WAE).

hide secret "hide" often substitutes for "keep" so that NE "hide secret" would be equivalent to BE "keep a secret", i.e. "not to tell it to anyone else", as in "Just tell me the truth. Don't hide any secret from me."

highlife ellipsis for "high-life music", a brand of music style combining jazz and West African elements, popular in Nigeria and other West African countries. In BE, "high life" denotes a style of life that involves spending a lot of money on entertainment, good food, expensive clothes, etc.

high/about time this phrase is sometimes followed by a present tense in NE, e.g. "It is high time we end this meeting." In BE, it has the meaning "the time is past when something should have happened or been done" and is always followed by a past tense, e.g. "It's high time you stopped fooling around and started looking for a job"; "Isn't it about time we were going?"

hip, hip, hip, hurrah in Nigeria, it is conventional for the person introducing this mode of cheers (in expression of delight, approval, thanks, etc.) to say "hip" three times. In Britain, it is said only two times.

hired assassins professional killers, who are often

hired to murder political opponents, perceived enemies or business rivals, as in "The former NFA boss was murdered by people suspected to be hired assassins."

His Royal Highness traditional rulers in Nigeria are usually addressed by this title, e.g. "His Royal Highness, the Obi of Onitsha."

hold there is a preference in NE for the active instead of the passive form of "hold" when the meaning indicated by the context is "take place", as in "The conference could not hold as planned because of the refusal of police to approve of it." BE uses "could not be held" and not "could not hold."

hollandies a two-piece waist cloth worn by women from buttocks down to their legs.

holy oil oil that is blessed and seen as sacred among some religious groups, e.g. "Since I realized the usefulness of holy oil, I always have it in my house."

holy water water blessed and seen to possess healing power in some religious circle, as in "Mr. Okorie had to sprinkle holy water all over his compound in order to disarm evil minded persons."

home people often used in NE to refer to one's relatives who live in the village otherwise known as "home town", as in "Greet the home people for me."

hometown "town" or the birth place of one's father (but not necessarily one's birth place) in which one has relations. One may even not have been there in one's

___

lifetime. In BE, "hometown" denotes a place where one was born or has lived for a long time.

home training "upbringing", as in "She lacks home training, and that is why she insults her husband in public." This would be equivalent to BE "She wasn't brought up well (by her parents), that is why she insults her husband in public."

home video name for plays and soaps acted by Nigerian actors and recorded on video cassettes, e.g. "Home video people gathered that not even the male actors were spared of this attack which began as fan adoration."

horn this word with the meaning "a device for sounding warning signal" is normally a noun in BE, e.g. "The car has a loud horn." In NE, "horn" is sometimes found as a verb, as in the notice of warning usually at the back of lorries, "Horn before overtake", or the sentence "I started horning right from the roundabout."

hot often collocates with head or body, particularly in the context of ill-health, e.g. "My body is very hot for Be "The temperature of my body is very high."

hot drink "hot drink" is a NE word for "alcoholic spirits", "liquor" such as gin, whisky, brandy, schnapps, etc. The word "drink" is sometimes omitted as in "I would like to take hot." (Also in WAE).

hotel the meaning is often extended in NE to cover BE "restaurant", "cafe" (not necessarily with lodging), "public house" and "brothel".

houseboy "house keeper". There is also "house-girl".

House of Assembly the legislative body of persons for every state in Nigeria (State House of Assembly) for which, members are chosen by political elections. The federal equivalent of this legislative body is known as House of Representatives.

house warming ceremony celebrations that usually follow the completion of a new house, as in "We attended Chief Duro's house warming ceremony yesterday."

how? ellipsis for "How are you?" Other forms of this greeting include "How now?", "How things?", "How far?", "How work?", "How life?", "How family?", etc.

How come? an interrogative meaning "How is it that?"; "Why?", e.g. "How come that you stayed away from work for one week without permission?"

how body? ellipsis from "How is your body?" equivalent to "How is the state of your health?"

How market? How is business?

HRVIC an acronym for Human Rights Violations Investigations Commission, which is also known as Oputa Panel.

hundred many NE speakers use the plural form of this noun with -s in contexts where BE speakers will use the singular form, e.g. "Several hundreds of people attended the rally" for BE "Several hundred people attended the rally"; "We still have a few hundreds of

---

criminals in this country" for BE "We still have a few hundred criminals in this country."

husband-snatcher name frequently called women who go out with other women's husbands, e.g. "She calls me husband-snatcher while she was the one who snatched my husband from me."

hut a small house usually a room which serves as a reception or guest room for an old man.

I

I am the one commonly used rather emphatically in response to a question wanting to know who took a particular action. It is equivalent to BE "I am", "I do" or "I did", e.g.:
A: Who took the money on top of the table?
B: I am the one.

I and you this order—"I and you"; "I and she"; "I and Udo"—is frequently used in NE, as in "I and you are one." In BE, the order is "You and I"; "She and I"; "Udo and I."

I wonder! often used in conversation as an interjection, which expresses strong agreement with a previous statement by another person, e.g.:
A: This lecturer likes failing students.
B: I wonder!

iba /iba/ jaundice, or jaundice-like fever; high fever associated with malaria; fever in general; red eye associated with fever, as in "Buy medicine for any form of iba." (SL: Igbo).

Ibo /ibo/ older and inaccurate form of 'Igbo', referring to Igbo people and Igbo language.

ice-block commonly used where BE uses "ice" or "ice-cubes", i.e. a small piece of ice for cooling drinks, etc., as in "Buy ice-block."

ice water this phrase, meaning water that has been iced for drinking (either with pieces of ice or by being refrigerated) is usually found in NE, e.g. "Buy ice water." Most speakers of BE would prefer to say "iced water" rather than "ice water". (Also in WAE).

idol worshippers a derogatory way by which Nigerian Christians and Moslems refer to those who practise African traditional religion, e.g. "Idol worshippers have been wasting their time because they are not worshipping a living God."

if by chance supposing; should; in case, e.g. "If by chance he comes, ask him to wait for me" for BE "Supposing he comes, ask him to wait for me."

ifa /ifa/ "oracle" or "divination", frequently used in NE, as in "The ifa priest asked him to come back the following day for more information about his future." (SL: Yoruba).

IFEM an acronym for Interbank Foreign Exchange Market.

IG an abbreviation for Inspector General of Police, the highest ranking officer of the Nigeria police force.

igba /igba/ traditional drum. (SL: Igbo).

igbo /igbo/ a slang for Indian hemp, as in "Before we left Lagos on any of our foreign tours, Fela would instruct everyone not to carry Indian hemp. This is because, according to him, the gospel he wanted to preach to the world is much greater than igbo."

Igbo /igbo/ name of one of the three major ethnic groups in Nigeria, as in "Igbo people"; a person of Igbo descent. It is also the name of the language spoken by the Igbo people, which is one of the indigenous official languages in Nigeria.

Igbo kwenu! frequently heard at occasions, meetings or parties involving the Igbo people of Nigeria, as a greeting, which usually precedes a speech.

Igbo-made /igbo meid/ often used colloquially for "fake products", as in "Please tell me the truth: is this shoe original or igbo-made?"

Igwe /igwe/ a title of honour, as in "Igwe of Ihiteowerri"; also name for the Sky God.

Ijaw /idʒɔ:/ an ethnic group in southern Nigeria found within the riverine areas of Edo, Delta, Ondo, Rivers and Bayelsa states, popular for fishing.

ikebe /ikebe/ often used colloquially to mean buttocks, especially in descriptions about women, e.g. "She has a very big ikebe." (SL: Pidgin).

Ikemba /ikemba/ a chieftaincy title as in "Ikemba Nnewi". (SL: Igbo).

ikenga /ikenga/ a symbol of strength among the Igbo; carved ritual figure with upraised right arm; carved wooden figure representing achievement and uprightness; symbol of personal worth, e.g. "In front of Abia State University lies a well-carved ikenga." (SL: Igbo).

ikolo /ikolo/ large slit drum, owned communally by a village or town, used to summon adults to important meetings, festivals or emergencies, as in "Mr. Ikenna was terrified at the sound of ikolo because the last time the ikolo was beaten, it was to announce the death of an important title holder." (SL: Igbo).

i/m an abbreviation for "ima mmadu" meaning "connection" or "undue influence", as in "I must make a good grade in my degree examination to be able to get a job since I don't have i/m." (SL: Igbo).

I'm coming a NE speaker says "I am coming" when, in fact, he is going away to come back soon. This is equivalent to BE "I will be back soon."

imagination the definite article "the" is frequently omitted in the NE idiomatic expression "not by any/ by no stretch of imagination," which is equivalent to BE "not by any/by no stretch of the imagination", meaning "however hard one may try to believe or imagine something", e.g. "By no stretch of imagination could anyone trust him" for BE "By no stretch of the imagination could anyone trust him."

imagine! an exclamation of surprise or disapproval over an action or a decision that has just been taken. Its variant form is "Just imagine!" equivalent to BE

"Imagine that!", "Fancy that!", e.g.:
A: I heard from the news this morning that Government has further increased the price of fuel.
B: Just imagine!

Imam an Islamic priest who leads the prayer at a congregation. (Arabic).

imitation sometimes used to mean "goods of inferior quality", as in "We don't sell imitation here."

impregnate a polite word for "put in a family way" or "make pregnant", which frequently occurs in both formal and informal styles, e.g. "He impregnated his wife before their wedding"; "Nwoye is old enough to impregnate a woman." It is more commonly used by less educated Nigerians. If at all "impregnate" is found in BE usage, it will be in formal style.

in as much as this is used with the meaning "because", "although", as in "In as much as you are my friend, I cannot do what is wrong for your sake."

incharge (of) formed in agglutination for BE 'in charge (of)'.

include in NE, "etceteras" is often used redundantly in the same sentence with "include", e.g. "Some of the departments in the faculty include English, Linguistics, Philosophy, Modern Languages, etc." In BE, "etc." will be omitted in this sentence and replaced by the conjunction "and" so that we would have a sentence such as "Some of the departments in the faculty include English, Linguistics, Philosophy, and Modern

Languages."

Independence Day Nigeria got its independence from the British rule on October 1, 1960, and so the independence day is celebrated every October 1.

indigenes natives of a state or local government area, as in "All the indigenes of Lagos state who are interested in enlistment into the Nigerian armed forces are requested to come for interview."

indiscipline NE users often inflect this word to past tense, probably in analogy with "discipline" and "disciplined", as in "It is widely believed that most university students are highly indisciplined." BE uses this word only as a noun and without the inflectional morpheme.

in good terms "in" replaces "on" in NE expression "in good terms with" which is equivalent to BE "on good terms with", i.e. having a relationship.

INEC acronym for Independent National Electoral . Commission—body charged with registration of parties as well as conducting of elections in the country.

infact many speakers of NE write these two words as one word, e.g. "Thanks for your useful suggestion. Infact, I have been thinking of it before your letter." In BE, they are usually written as two different words, "in fact".

ING abbreviation for Interim National Government, which was put in place by the Babangida administration after the annulment of June 12 election.

Insha Allah this expression is frequently used in the northern part of Nigeria to mean "By the grace of God", as in "We have the best players who are playing for big teams and all I can say is that with your support, insha Allah, we will win in France." (SL: Hausa).

inspite like "in fact", many speakers of NE write these two words as one word, perhaps in confusion with "despite", e.g. "Inspite of being an oil-producing area, the community lacks basic amenities such as good roads, good drinking water and even electricity."

installment often used with an adverbial suffix in NE, e.g. "He accepted to pay the remaining money installmentally" for BE "He accepted to pay the remaining money in installments."

interested "to be interested in somebody" also means "to fall in love" with that person, as in "Akin is interested in Oluchi."

into in the register of mathematics, "into" is frequently used to denote "multiplication" in NE, as in "Two into six is twelve." In BE, it denotes "division" so that "Two into six" will be three.

invited dignitaries the modifier "invited" will be redundant in BE but not in NE where "invited dignitaries" or "invited guests" are frequently used, as in "All the invited dignitaries should please come into the hall." "Invited" is considered redundant in BE because dignitaries will have to be invited to an occasion for them to attend.

invitee frequently used in NE, but not in BE, to mean "guests" in an occasion, as in "Invitees who have gifts for the couple can now come forward with them." "Invitee" is derived from "invite" in analogy with existing English words.

inyanga /iɲanga/ being unduly proud; to be impressive or to behave in a manner as to attract attention to oneself, as in "That girl is always making inyanga. Does she think that everybody has the time to look at her?"; "The fact is that Obiageli had been making inyanga with her pot." It is sometimes written as 'yanga'. (SL: Pidgin).

iroko /iroko/ tall, huge, hardwood of mulberry tree. (SL: Yoruba).

is this your face? frequently used to express surprise that one has not been seen for a long time. It may be equivalent to BE "Where have you been since?"

isiagu /isiagʋ/ a long flowing top made of velvet material with lion's head designed all over the material, which is sometimes won along with a wrapper or a pair of trousers, popular among the Igbo, e.g. "I have always wanted to buy isiagu." (SL: Igbo).

isi-ewu /isiewu/ a delicacy made from the head of a goat. See "goat-head". (SL: Igbo).

issue NE often treats "issue" as a countable noun, i.e. when it denotes "children of one's own" or "offspring", e.g. "We already have four issues, though they are all females." BE uses the singular form and strictly in formal context, as in "He died without issue."

isn't it? NE speakers use this tag very frequently in contexts where BE would use a different tag, e.g. "You have been here before, isn't it?" In BE, this question tag is only found when the sentence preceding the tag has a neuter subject and includes the verb "to be", e.g. "The party is after work, isn't it?"

it remains left; still left; commonly occurs before a noun phrase in response to questions about number, e.g.:
A: How many bags of rice do you have?
B: It remains ten bags.
"It remains" is used in NE where BE would use "There remain(s)" or "There are only."

it's a pity in BE, "It's a pity" functions as an antecedent to a relative clause beginning with "that", e.g. "It's a pity that you failed my course." In NE, "It's a pity" may be used as an independent expression of sympathy to one who has suffered some misfortune, e.g.:
A: Is it true that armed robbers came to your compound last night?
B: Yes.
A: It's a pity.

item seven frequently used to refer to food service as the last item on the agenda of a ceremony.

iyan /iɲɔ/ a meal of pounded yam. (SL: Yoruba).

iyawo /ijawo/ primarily means "wife", but frequently used to address married women in the sense of "madam". (SL: Yoruba).

J

JAMB an acronym for Joint Admissions and Matriculation Board, a body that conducts entrance examinations into Nigerian universities and other higher institutions.

jambite coined from Joint Admissions and Matriculations Board (JAMB), it is frequently used in universities to refer to first year students who have just been admitted into universities after passing the University Matriculation Examinations (UME), as in "All jambites are requested to report to the central administration on Monday morning for registration."

jara /dʒara/ the little extra quantity given free of charge to a customer over and above the quantity for which he has paid, as in "Madam, put jara." It may be loosely equivalent to "discount", although it is in form of additional quantity. (SL: Hausa).

jealous often used as a verb in NE, e.g. "I don't jealous you"; "My attitude doesn't mean I am jealousing you" instead of "I don't envy you"; "My attitude doesn't mean I am jealous of you."

jealousing jealous of, e.g. "Why are you jealousing me?" for BE "Why are you jealous of me?"

jedijedi /dʒedidʒedi/ a Yoruba term for "pile" which has found currency in NE, as in "This medicine cures jedijedi instantly." (SL: Yoruba).

jerry-can a 25-litre container

jesu /dʒeːsu/ a clipped form of "Jesus".

jewellery this noun is often found in the plural in NE, as in "She spends all her money on jewelleries." This noun is treated as a non-count in BE and so "jewellery" will be preferred in the sentence above.

jigger a disease that attacks the foot believed to be caused by pigs, and known for causing jigging or very irritating discomfort, e.g. "The Oba has banned the rearing of pigs in his domain because of wide spread of jigger in the area."

jihad Islamic term for holy war or righteous struggle, e.g. "Police have uncovered plans by the members of Maitasine sect to launch a jihad in the Lagos areas." (SL: Arabic).

JJC an abbreviation for John Just Come, a slang commonly used among students for "newcomer" to a school, club, city, etc. It is also used to mean "learner", as in "Go away from the road, you learner, JJC."

jo /dʒɔː/ "please" frequently used in NE, especially by the Yoruba people, e.g. "Leave me jo" for BE "Please leave me." (SL: Yoruba).

join frequently collocates with a transport system in traveling context to mean "travel by" or "go by" , as in "join bus", "join a taxi", "join plane". "Join" is also used in NE as an ellipsis for BE "Join the staff of ", as in "He joined the university in 1988 as a graduate assistant" for "He joined the staff of the university in 1988 as a graduate assistant."

join army a common collocation for "enlist" e.g. "His elder brother joined army two years ago" for BE "His elder brother enlisted as a soldier two years ago."

joke a NE idiomatic expression, "Joke with fire" is equivalent to BE "play with fire", i.e. "to take foolish and dangerous risks", e.g. "Don't joke with fire" for BE "Don't play with fire."

jolof "rice porridge", i.e. rice cooked together with every necessary ingredient. Jolof rice is different from rice cooked without ingredients and eaten with stew, e.g. "Where is the pot containing the corned beef jolof rice cooked for the Pastor?"

JSSCE an abbreviation for Junior Secondary School Certificate Examination, an examination conducted by West African School Certificate Examination after three years of secondary education, e.g. "The Nigeria Union of Teachers (NUT) had threatened to boycott the August 31 JSSCE in Kwara state, if the government does not rescind its decision to retire secondary school teachers with 30 years of service experience."

juggernaut used in political context to mean an influential politician, e.g. "May I introduce to you a man of timber and calibre and a political juggernaut, Chief

Kingsley Mbadiwe."

juju /dʒudʒu/ 1. talisman, idol, witch-craft, poison, charm, as in "They killed the former pastor with juju." 2. a popular Nigerian music, "juju music", popularized by Ebenener Obey and Sunny Ade. (SL: Yoruba).

jumat prayer Muslim prayer held every Friday, as in "According to the Sultan, Moslems oppose the recent announcements asking them to return to work after the Jumat prayers on Friday." (SL: Arabic).

jumbo sale "jumbo" substitutes for "jumble" in the NE idiomatic expression "Jumbo sale" which is equivalent to BE "jumble sale", meaning "a sale of a mixed collection of old things that are no longer wanted in order to raise money, usually for charity." However, the NE idiom "jumbo sale" refers to "very large sale", as in "Last December, traders in Onitsha main market had a jumbo sale."

jumper in NE, a "jumper" usually refers to a tunic made of cotton, and reaching from the neck to the waist. In BE, a "jumper" is "a garment of knitted wool or cotton without fastenings, usually worn over a shirt or blouse."

June 12 used frequently to refer to pro democracy day to commemorate the annulment of a presidential election won by Chief Moshood Abiola. It is also seen as a remarkable date that reminds Nigerians of unwillingness on the part of the military to hand over power, e.g. "General Babangida took Nigeria on a serpentine transition programme for eight solid years that resulted in the June 12 imbroglio."

June Twelver an apostle of the actualization of June 12 presidential election believed to have been won by Chief M.K.O. Abiola, but which was annulled by the military in 1993, as in "All June twelvers have been advised to forget the past so that the country can move forward."

junior brother meaning "younger brother", as in "My junior brother had just graduated from the university."

just many speakers of NE use double adverbial constructions involving "just" and "only" for emphasis, e.g. "Bring just only one." This would not be encountered very often in BE.

just close your eyes and to do something without a second thought, as in "Just close your eyes and do it for her" for BE "Do it for her without a second thought."

K

Kabiyesi /kabiesi/ a royal title and greeting to a Yoruba king. (SL: Yoruba).

kabukabu /kabukabu/ an unlicensed taxi or private cars carrying passengers illegally, common in large cities, as in "Many civil servants across the nation now use their cars for kabukabu in order to make ends meet." (SL: Yoruba).

Kaduna mafia frequently found in Nigeria's political idiom referring to a coalition of highly influential northern politicians, businessmen and soldiers with overwhelming control on the politics of Nigeria.

kaftan /kafta:n/ a long gown worn mostly by men, as in "His richly embroidered kaftan and hand-made hat became him well." (SL: Hausa).

kai! /kai/ an interjection that expresses strong surprise. (SL: Hausa).

kaikai /kaikai/ a local gin distilled from the fermented sap of the raffia palm. (SL: Ijaw?).

kalabule /kalabule/ black market. (SL: Yoruba).

kalakuta republic also known as "African shrine", it is the name for the house where the popular Nigerian musician, Fela Anikulapo Kuti lived and conducted his musical concerts, as in "Beko drove straight from the Murtala Muhammed Airport, Ikeja to the Kalakuta Republic on Gbemisola street, Ikeja to pay his last respects to the legendary Afrobeat king."

Kanuri /kanuri/ a small ethnic group in northern Nigeria.

katakata /katakata/ "riots", as in "Everybody is worried about what will happen in Nigeria this year. Let us hope there will not be katakata in Lagos streets." (SL: Pidgin).

ke /ke/ commonly used for emphasis, as in "True love is a serious matter ke." (SL: Yoruba).

kedu? /kedu/ a common greeting, particularly, among the Igbo, meaning "How are you?" (SL: Igbo).

keep sometimes used in NE where BE would prefer "put", e.g. "Keep the book on my table" for BE "Put the book on my table."

kerosene the NE word for what is known as "paraffin" in BE. This must have been part of the influence of the American English.

khaki thick clothing material used in sewing military uniform.

Khaki boys derogatorily used for military men, as in "The country was making steady progress until khaki boys intruded into the nation's political life."

kia-kia bus /kiakia bʌs/ a Volkswagen bus with the capacity for a very high speed on Nigerian roads. It is also known as kombi bus.

kick a car "to kick a car" is a NE expression often used to mean "to start a car", as in "Kick the car while I push it."

kick against commonly occurs in both formal and informal styles in NE, with the meaning "protest against", "resist", e.g. "The Non-Academic Staff Union of Universities (NASU) told the government representatives that they are not against salary increase in the universities but that they are only kicking against the introduction of disparities in salaries between ASUU and NASU members." In BE, "kick against" occurs only in informal style.

kickback frequently used in NE to mean payment to government officials for contracts awarded, as in "After collecting kickbacks from the contractors, the Minister did nothing to ensure that the project was completed." "Kickback" is also used in BE but only in informal style, with the meaning "money paid to somebody who has helped one to make a profit, often illegally."

kilo a clipped form of "kilogramme". Unlike BE, NE often uses it as a measure of distance and weight.

kiss "kiss" substitutes for "bite" in the NE idiomatic expression "kiss the dust" which is equivalent to BE "bite the dust", meaning "to be defeated", as in "Bash Ali accused the judges of bias in a fight in which he kissed the dust in Germany."

k-leg of legs not very straight; deformed, e.g. "The man with k-leg called yesterday."

knickers "knickers" in NE refers to "men's shorts or underpants." In BE, "knickers" denotes a woman's or girl's undergarment worn under other clothes and covering the body from the waist to the tops of the legs. The singular form "knicker" is often found in NE (as in "Has anybody seen my black knicker?") where BE usage would accept "a pair of knickers" (as in "Has anybody seen a pair of my black knickers"). Also found in NE but not in BE, particularly at the lower educational level, is "short knicker" for BE "knickers" or American English "shorts."

knockout fire-crackers, banger or any of the noisy fireworks commonly used particularly by children during Christmas and New Year celebrations, as in "Many youths in the Ogun state capital, Abeokuta, spent the New Year's day in police cells for exploding knockouts, which the law enforcement agencies said were banned."

know often used to collocate with "book" to mean "be intelligent", as in "I don't know book" for BE "I am not intelligent."

kobo /kɔbɔ/ a unit of money in Nigeria. 100 kobo make up one Naira.

koboko /koboko/ "horsewhip", i.e. a big, strong whip commonly used for the cow, e.g. "Their koboko whips crackled and whistled menacingly as they cracked them repeatedly"; "If it requires giving you 25 lashes, I would whip you with koboko." (SL: Hausa).

kobo kobo /kobokobo/ an informal, often humorous name which the Yorubas of Southwestern Nigeria call the Igbos of Southeastern Nigeria. "Kobo kobo" literally means "people who wear loincloths." (SL: Yoruba).

kola /kola/ 1. edible seed of the kola tree, highly valued in Nigeria as a traditional gift usually presented to guests.
2. a clipped form of "kolanut". The meaning is often extended to include drinks or anything that can be presented to guests, as in "I'm sorry I don't have any kola to present to you."
3. among the law enforcement agents like the Nigeria Police, "kola" refers to "bribe" or some money expected in return for favour done to one, as in "Officer, please help me. I will give you some kola."

kombi bus /kombi bʌs/ same as "kia-kia bus", i.e. a Volkswagen minibus.

kpatakpata /kpatakpata/ everything; completely, e.g. "It has finished kpatakpata" for BE "It has finished completely." (SL: Pidgin).

kpomo /kpɔmɔ/ frequently used in Edo and Delta states to refer to cow skin or leather prepared to be eaten, e.g. "I know that kpomo has no nutritional value, but I still eat it." See also ponmo. (SL: Edo).

kunu /kwunu/ soft drink prepared from millet or guinea corn. (SL: Hausa).

kwashiokor protein deficiency disease common during the Nigerian civil war.

L

lack respect disrespectful, as in "The boy lacks respect" for BE "The boy is disrespectful."

lady 1. often used as a mode of address perceived to be more dignifying than "woman" or "girl", e.g. "I addressed her as a woman but she said she is a lady and not a woman."
2. a female who is old enough to be married but still single. In this sense, she is older than a "girl" but cannot be regarded as a woman because she is not yet married.

Lagosian one from the Lagos State of Nigeria, as in "I am a Lagosian"; "Although the movements of the bespectacled 56-year old general were not announced in advance, thousands of Lagosians tried to greet him at the airport as he shuttled between installations in the south of the country, which has long opposed military rule."

lailai /lailai/ at all; never, as in "I will never accept that decision lailai."

land frequently used in interrupted speech to mean "explaining a point more clearly", e.g. when a speaker says "Please let me land", he aims at getting the attention of his disagreeing audience in order to thoroughly explain his point.

lap this noun is often pluralized in NE where BE retains the singular form, e.g. "I don't allow men to sit on my laps"; "Why don't you keep the basket in the booth instead of carrying it on your laps." In the two examples, BE would normally use the singular form.

lappa /lapa/ "wrapper" or "waist-cloth", i.e. one or two-piece cloth used mainly by women, e.g. "This is because the Igbo belief was that a complete woman must have two lappas round her waist, not just one." (SL: Pidgin).

lassa fever a highly infectious viral disease with such symptoms as high fever, internal hemorrhage and heart infection, and caused by contact with an infected mouse.

last 1. an ellipsis for "last price", and it is frequently used in market bargaining by a buyer or seller to indicate the final acceptable price, as in "Ten Naira last." This expression is absent in BE because the kind of bargaining that usually gives rise to it is lacking in Britain.
2. ellipsis for "last long", e.g. "The film did not last" for BE "The film did not last long."

last-born commonly used in NE to describe the youngest child in the family, e.g. "My father's last-born is fifteen years old."

last but not the least the definite article "the" is often added in the NE expression "last but not the least" which is equivalent to BE "last but not least", i.e. "last but no less important than the others", e.g. "And last but not the least is the perennial water problem in this state"; "Last but not the least, I would like to thank my good friend Kenny Popoola."

last week Sunday often used as an equivalent to BE "last Sunday". The inclusion of "week" will be considered redundant in BE.

late 1. sometimes used in NE in the predicative, meaning "deceased", "dead", e.g. "His father is late" for BE "His father is dead." In BE, the adjective "late" is used attributively to describe a person who is dead, as in "her late husband."
2. frequently used in describing a wrist watch or clock that is showing time later than the correct time, e.g. "My watch is two minutes late" will be equivalent in BE to "My watch is two minutes slow."

latrine in BE, the use of "latrine" is restricted in that it denotes "a toilet in a camp, barracks, etc., especially one made by digging a hole in the ground." Such restriction in meaning does not often apply in NE, especially at the lower educational level. The NE expression, "I am going to the latrine" is also understood to mean "I am going to the toilet."

law the determiner "own" is often omitted in the NE idiomatic expression "take the law into one's hands" which is equivalent to BE "take the law into one's own hands", i.e. "to act independently, often using force, to punish somebody who has done something wrong", as in "Police have warned Nigerians to desist from taking the law into their hands." In BE usage, the determiner "own" will be added in this idiomatic construction.

leak orange eat some orange, as in "Emeka is leaking some orange" for BE "Emeka is eating some orange."

lean in NE, "lean" is frequently used pejoratively, especially in the context of illness to mean "emaciated", as in "You should eat very well to recover fully from your illness, you look very lean." When "lean" is used in BE in reference to people, it denotes "thin and fit", as in "a thin athletic body."

leather bag less educated speakers of NE sometimes use "leather bag" to mean BE "plastic bag". A leather bag should be made of animal skin, while a "plastic bag" should be made of plastic material. This distinction is often ignored in NE.

leave sometimes used in NE to mean "stop" or "discontinue". For instance, when a NE speaker says "I have left her", what he intends to imply is that he has discontinued a relationship with her. "Leave" is not used in this sense in BE. Another common use of "leave" in NE is its collocation with "behind" where "behind" will be considered redundant in BE, e.g. "The Chief died in the early hours of Saturday, leaving behind his wife and six children."

leg this noun is often found with the plural -s in the NE idiomatic expression "pull somebody's legs" which is equivalent to BE "pull somebody's leg", i.e. "to play a joke on somebody, especially by making him/her believe something that is not true", e.g. "Don't mind him—he was only pulling your legs." In BE idiomatic expression, the singular form of this noun is used.

legal practitioner frequently used in NE as a way of describing one qualified to practise law as a "barrister" and "solicitor". In Britain, but not in Nigeria, the functions of a "barrister" and a "solicitor" are separated between different persons. This means that a lawyer is practising either as a "barrister" or a "solicitor" in Britain but not as a "legal practitioner", as done in Nigeria.

lend the particle "out" often follows "lend" in contexts where the particle will not be found in BE, e.g. "The lecturer said that he had lent out the book to a student." The particle "out" would be considered redundant by BE speakers.

lesson frequently used to mean "private tuition", as in "I understand mathematics better from our lesson teacher than in school." In BE, "lesson" denotes a period of time given to learning or teaching, or a class, as in "English lesson."

let the "to" infinitive is often found after "let" in NE usage but not in BE, e.g. "She wants to leave the company but her boss won't let her to go." In BE, the "to" infinitive is normal after "allow" but is never found after "let", e.g. "She wanted to lend me some money but I wouldn't let her do it."

let-my-people-go slang commonly used in Nigerian universities to describe the lowest pass grade, usually from 40% to 49%, as in "The lecturer gave me let-my-people-go"; "However, the responses from the other contestants were not extraordinarily brilliant either. They were more like 'let-my-people-go kind of answers'."

lift frequently found in the register of sports writing in Nigeria where BE would prefer "win", e.g. "Shooting Stars will be winning the cup for keeps having lifted it the previous year."

LGA an abbreviation for Local Government Area—an administrative area, as in "The chairman advised all the teachers in Orlu L.G.A. to be more dedicated to their duty."

light also commonly used to mean "electricity", as in "We have not had light for the past three days". In BE, "electricity" is only a source of light—"the natural force that makes things visible."

like "like" often collocates with "money", as in "She likes money a lot", a NE idiomatic expression, equivalent to BE "She is very conscious of money."

like I have been saying as I had said earlier, e.g. "Like I have been saying, you have to work hard" for BE "As I had earlier said, you have to work hard."

like that 1. often used in conversation where BE would use "a certain", e.g.:
A: Do you still recognise me?
B: Yes, were you not the person that came to our house one Sunday like that?

"One Sunday like that" would in BE be "One certain Sunday."

2. a frequently used collocation referring to something strange or to a stranger, e.g. "I saw one man like that" for BE "I saw a strange man"; "It just happened like that" for BE "It occurred strangely."

like this 1. worried, as in "Why are you looking like this?" for BE "What is the matter?"

2. very; unreliable, e.g. "Why are you wicked like this?" for BE "Why are you very wicked?"; "Why are you behaving like this?" for BE "Why do you appear to be unreliable?"

Lipton Lipton is a popular brand of tea, but there is a tendency in NE to refer to all brands of tea as Lipton. For instance, when a buyer says "Do you have Lipton?" he may have in mind any tea of the brand of Lipton.

list the adverbial particle "down" is often found after "list" in NE, as in "I want every student to list down only the main points." Most BE speakers would consider this particle to be redundant in this sentence.

load there is the tendency in NE to inflect this noun for plural when used to mean "belongings", as in "The landlord asked him to pack his loads and leave his house." In BE, "load" represents the total number or amount and so is not used with the plural -s. In another sense, the meaning of load is often extended in NE to mean "luggage", as in "Where is your load?" for BE "Where is your luggage?"

local in BE, "local" has the meaning, "belonging or relating to a particular place or district", e.g. "a local doctor", "a local farmer", etc. In NE, "local" is frequently used to describe a person, his character, or ideas to mean "primitive", "uncivilized", "unrefined", or "parochial" depending on the context, e.g. "She is a very local girl" may mean that the girl looks unrefined. "His village is too local" may suggest that his village lacks amenities.

lock the particle "up" often follows "lock" in contexts where it will not be found in BE, e.g. "Please remember to lock up the gate before leaving." In BE, this particle will be considered redundant in the above sentence. However, "lock up" may be found in such sentences as "The jewellery was locked up in a safe" (where it means to store something in a safe place), and "Don't forget to lock up before leaving home" (where it means to make a house, etc. secure by locking the doors and windows).

locust bean seasoning or spices made from fermented locust bean used for food preparation. It is known in Hausa as dawadawa, iru in Yoruba, and ogiri in Igbo.

log of wood there is an unnecessary repetition of 'log' and 'wood' in NE but not in BE, e.g. "He sleeps like a log of wood" for BE "He sleeps like a log" or "He sleeps like a mass of wood."

Long juju also known as Ibini Ukpabi, it is name for the oracle of the Aro people, which was effectively utilized for the benefit of slave trade.

long-leg "undue influence" or nepotism, as in "Only those with long leg get good jobs."

long-throat "covetousness", "greed", as in "She has long throat over meat."

look often used in NE where BE would prefer 'search', e.g. "I am looking for my book" for BE "I am searching for my book."

look somehow a commonly heard expression in NE is "Your face looks somehow" for BE "You seem unhappy."

lorry-park a large area set aside for only lorries to load and off-load. This may be equivalent to "lorry stations" in BE.

lost and found the conjunction "and" sometimes substitutes for "but" in the NE expression "lost and found" which is equivalent to BE "lost but found."

low-cut hair style usually cut very low. "She is always wearing a low-cut, and I think it fits her."

luggage this noun is non-count in BE and so does not occur in the plural form or with an indefinite article, as often observed in NE, e.g. "Luggages are at the owners risk"; "I have only a luggage."

luxurious ellipsis for "luxurious bus", which is equivalent to BE "luxury bus", i.e. a long bus frequently used for long distant journeys, as in "I always travel from Lagos to Onitsha by luxurious."

M

ma a clipped form of "mama", used as a title of respect for very old women, especially among the Yorubas and Bendelites. This title is usually followed by her last name, as in "Ma Odeshi."

Maazi /maazi/ title for head of settlement among the Aro; used (originally) to refer only to distinguished free-born adult men, equivalent to 'Lord' or 'Sir' in European usage; general title of reverence for men of substance; used for the title "Mr." among the Igbo, as in "Mazi Ogbalu." (SL: Igbo).

machet "machet" is a broad heavy knife used as a cutting tool and as a weapon. But it is often found in NE as a verb, e.g. "While the looting was going on, a Nigerian Ports Authority night watchman who tried to escape from the scene was macheted to death."

machine frequently used to mean "motorcycle", as in "He has a machine in the village". "Machine" is also often used to mean "sewing machine". In BE, "sewing-machine" is just one type of machine.

machinery this noun is normally treated as non-count in BE and is rarely found in the plural form as is often used in NE, e.g. "When this industry takes off fully, it

---

will be manufacturing machineries of all kinds."

maclean "maclean" is a popular brand of toothpaste, but it is often used to refer to toothpaste in general so that when a buyer asks for "maclean", he may have in mind any toothpaste familiar to him.

madaki /madaki/ traditional chieftaincy title in Bauchi, as in "The Madaki of Bauchi." (SL: Hausa).

madam in BE, "madam" is used formally as a polite form of address to a woman that one does not know, whether she is married or not. "Madam" is primarily used in NE as a mode of address to a married woman. Another common use of this term is manifested in this frequently heard question "What of madam?" for BE "How is your wife?" "Madam" is also often used to refer to a woman who has domestic servants or a woman who is head of an establishment, as in "Our madam had just gone out" for BE "Our boss had just gone out." This sense is certainly different from the use of "madam" as a mode of address. (Also in WAE).

mago-mago /mago mago/ dishonesty, favouritism, as in "No wonder why some mago mago was done in the boardroom to ensure that Plateau United played in the Super League."

magun /magu/ a spell cast on a woman (suspected to be promiscuous) by her husband. The spell is usually placed on the ground and as soon as the woman crosses over it, any man with whom she indulges in extra marital sex will die through several means, which include somersaulting three times, sticking the woman's organ together with that of the man, and vomiting on the woman till death, as in "Pandemonium yesterday broke out in Gbagada police station as people scrambled to see a man and woman, who had their private parts glued together as a result of magun." (SL: Yoruba).

mai guard /me ga:d/ private security personnel; name popularly called day or night guards who are of Hausa origin. Mai guards are known to use bow and arrow for their security job, e.g. "If you want to sleep peacefully, you must have a mai guard."

make the use of 'to' infinitive after this verb is common in NE, as in "She made her husband to be wicked." BE would, in this sentence, use the base form without "to", i.e. "She made her husband wicked."

mainman a slang commonly used in universities to address one who does some favour to another, as in "You 're my mainman."

make face idiomatically used to mean "brag", "show-off" or "to behave in such a manner that calls for apologies from one", e.g. "You are always making face as if everybody is interested in you."

male issue often used in NE to mean "male child". In Nigeria, as in many African countries, emphasis is usually placed on the male child because the female child is seen as a temporary member of the family who will soon be married into a different family, e.g. "The former minister had to marry a second wife because the first marriage did not produce a male issue."

mallam a learned man, teacher, or a Muslim diviner commonly found among the Hausa, as in "Some of the politicians consult the mallams for protection." It is also often used, particularly in northern Nigeria, as title for a Muslim who has not been to Mecca on holy pilgrimage, as in "Sorry I am not an Alhaji yet. I am still a mallam." Also, the word "mallam" is frequently used as a popular NE slang for hair-cut that involves shaving off every hair completely, e.g. "I hope there is nothing wrong as you are wearing a mallam hair-cut." (SL: Arabic).

mama also used as a mode of address for older women (who may not be one's relatives) usually by younger people. "Mama" is also prefixed to the name of one's child as an address of respect, so that "Mama Iyabo", meaning "the mother of Iyabo" may be used as a polite form of address to Iyabo's mother. The same meaning applies to papa.

mammy wagon /mami wagɔn/ a kind of heavy-duty vehicle, used in carrying passengers, e.g. "It was quite a heavy downpour, the type that would stop in less than an hour, though to wait for it to stop would mean missing his mammy-wagon." Although used and mentioned extensively in the literature, it is probably now obsolete.

mammy water /mami wɔːtɔ/ "a mythical mermaid" believed to be living in the river, as in "Her nocturnal disappearances had mystified all of them until a dibia (herbalist) later claimed it was the work of Mammy Water, and outlined the rituals for freeing her."

man used colloquially for emphasis, as in "Man, I will be there immediately." It is often redundantly attached to names by friends as a mode of address that shows intimacy, e.g. "John man", also "Man John". In another sense, the statement "be man enough (to do something)" is frequently found in NE with the meaning "to be bold", "courageous enough."

man-eater used to describe one who eats human flesh. This expression became popularly used in the Nigerian press following the arrest of one Clifford Orji, a lunatic accused of eating human flesh, e.g. "Man-eater refuses to talk"; "Another man-eater found in Abeokuta."

man must wack a popular NE saying is "Man must wack", denoting a desperate survival effort; A man must live (eat) by whatever means, as in "The financial expert remarked that with the neglect of public schools by the government, the 'man must wack syndrome' leaves the teachers with the only option of combining their legitimate duties with petty trading and thereby neglecting their primary assignment."

manage 1. it is frequently used intransitively in greeting to suggest that one is only surviving in a difficult manner, e.g.:
A. "How is your family?"
B. "We are managing." The BE equivalent is "We are just existing."

2. it is also frequently used with the extended meaning "make a temporary use of something which is not functioning properly", as in "I knew that my tyre was bad, but I had to manage it to Aba since I didn't have a spare tyre in my car."

mangala /mangala/ species of dried fish, popular in the Eastern part of Nigeria.

many-many commonly used colloquially to mean "very many", as in "There were many-many people in the stadium during last week's league action."

march commonly occurs in NE in contexts where BE uses "tread", e.g. "Yesterday night, her grandmother marched on a small snake." In BE usage, the verb "tread" will be more appropriate in this sentence because "march" always takes place deliberately while "tread" may be accidental.

marginalization neglect, unfair treatment. In Nigeria, there are arbitrary and never-ending complaints of "marginalization." Every group in Nigeria claims to be "marginalized" in one form or another, e.g. "This is the real northern marginalization, even if subtle, but clearly using the instrumentality of a northerner."

market in Nigeria, a "market" is usually an open space where shopping is made, and so an utterance like "She has gone to the market" is commonly used where BE would use "She has gone for shopping."

market women a popular NE collocation used to refer to a social group of small scale traders who usually stay in the open market, e.g. "The radical Lagos lawyer said he expects students, market women and professional groups to be represented."

marriage many NE speakers use "marriage" and "wedding" as synonyms, e.g. "Their marriage took place last Saturday"; "A friend invited me to his daughter's marriage." In these sentences, BE speakers would prefer "wedding", i.e. "marriage ceremony and the party which usually follows it."

marriage engagement also known as "engagement ceremony" among the Yoruba and "traditional marriage" among other ethnic groups in Nigeria, "marriage engagement" is often used to describe traditional marriage ceremony which is different from the "church wedding", e.g. "I don't even know whether this is a marriage engagement or a political meeting."

marry sometimes used in the progressive form with the meaning "got married to", e.g. "She is an Igbo woman but she is marrying a Yoruba man." "...she is marrying a Yoruba man" is equivalent to BE "...she got married to a Yoruba man" or "...she married a Yoruba man."

may probably sometimes found in NE but not in BE, e.g. "Williams may probably travel to Jos tomorrow." Both "may" and "probably" suggest probability and cannot occur together in BE.

masquerade denotes an ancestral spirit, believed to dwell under the earth from where it emerges through

ant holes when the occasion arises, e.g. "She warned
the two boys not to cross the path of any real
masquerade." In BE, "masquerade" as a noun denotes
"an action, a manner, etc. that appears to be genuine or
sincere but is not", e.g. "Her sorrow is just a
masquerade."

matrimonial home a frequently heard collocation in
NE especially in relation to matrimonial problems, e.g.
"The man has packed out of his matrimonial home and
he is now living in one of the offices in his clinic."

May Day workers' day marked every 1st May, as in
"In his address at a rally to mark the May Day, the
Labour and Productivity Minister called on Nigerian
workers to support the transition program of the
government."

mature while NE uses it as a verb in the past tense
"matured", the BE uses the ordinary adjective "mature",
e.g. "He is searching for a girl who is fully matured for
marriage"; "Dan is not matured enough to drive a car."

mean this word is often found in contexts in NE where
it will not be found in BE, such as "How you mean? for
"What do you mean?"; "You mean to say ..." for "Do
you mean to say that ..."

mechanic's workshop coinage for "garage", i.e. a place
where repairs of vehicles are carried out, as in "My
daddy went to the mechanic's workshop. He will soon
be back."

---

medicated glasses frequently used to refer to any glasses prescribed by an optician in contrast with "sunshades", as in "He has been wearing medicated glasses for the past ten years." "Medicated glasses" is equivalent to "glasses" or "spectacles" in BE.

medicine-man often used in NE for BE "clairvoyant". A "medicine-man" combines the functions of a fortune-teller, a sooth-sayer, and a herbalist or a healer, e.g. "We were just returning from a medicine-man over my mother's sickness suspected to be poison"; "He surrounded himself with strong medicine-men who ended up deceiving him."

mediocre sometimes occurs in the plural form in NE, e.g. "The government of N.P.N. is dominated by mediocres." This noun occurs only in the singular form in BE.

meet often extended to mean "find", as in "I don't know the owner of that pen. I met it there when I came in." In BE "found" rather than "met" would be used in the above sentence. The same extension often occurs in the collocation of "meet" with "absence", as in "I came to your office and met your absence." "Meet" is also found in some contexts in NE where BE would prefer "see", as in "Let us go and meet the lecturer in his office." In BE, two persons "meet" by coming together in the same place.

men of the underworld popularly used in NE to refer to "armed robbers" or "criminals", as in "Men of the underworld struck again in the early hours of yesterday killing three people in Lagos." This expression has long become a cliché in BE.

men of timber and caliber Nigeria's political idiom, meaning "political heavyweights", as in "Chief K. O. Mbadiwe was a man of timber and caliber."

mention a frequently occurring expression in NE is "Don't mention" which is equivalent to BE "Don't mention it", used to indicate that thanks or apologies are not necessary, as in:
A: Thanks for the gift.
B: Don't mention.
Also, in NE, the particle "about" often follows the verb "mention" in contexts where the particle will not occur in BE, e.g. "Hasn't he mentioned about me to you before?" The particle "about" will be considered redundant by BE speakers.

mess up disgrace, e.g. "The department is not happy with you because you messed up everybody during your presentation."

midnight "Midnight" which in BE means "12 o'clock at night" is often used erroneously in a prepositional phrase beginning with "in" to mean "the middle of the night", as in "I like reading in the midnight", where BE would say "I like reading in the middle of the night."

mighty frequently used to describe the size of, especially, buildings, as in "He has a very mighty house in his village." "Mighty" is here used where BE would prefer "huge". In BE, "mighty" denotes "powerful", "strong", "great" and "impressive".

MILAD an acronym for "military administrator" which is equivalent to "governor" (of a state) in a democratic government, and popularly used by the media under military government, as in "Sources in Owerri informed TEMPO that the former MILAD himself may soon be summoned by the court to come and answer to the charges against him."

miliki /miliki/ "fun", "celebration", "enjoyment". (SL: Yoruba).

mind often used as a form of warning in the expression, "Mind yourself", which may be equivalent to "BE "Be careful" or "Watch it" or "Don't provoke me into losing my temper", e.g. "Please mind yourself." The occurrence of this expression may be an extension of the imperative in BE "Mind your own business", meaning "not to interfere in other people's affairs." In this BE expression, "own" is often omitted in NE version "Mind your business." "Mind" is also frequently used in the NE expression, "Don't mind him/her", meaning, "Don't pay attention to him/her." This NE usage may be an extension of BE, "If you don't mind", a polite request meant to confirm somebody's agreement with what is intended.

mineral commonly used to mean "soft drinks" such as Coca-Cola, Fanta, Sprite, etc., as in "Let me have mineral." (Also in WAE).

mmanwu /mmawu/ masquerade; masked dancer; masked spirit, e.g. "Mmanwu is still seen as a spirit in most Igbo traditional communities."

mmanwu festival /mmawu festivəl/ a festival in some parts of Igboland featuring masquerades. (SL: Igbo).

mobilization fee this phrase is commonly found in NE to denote the initial amount of money paid to contractors before they begin to execute contracts awarded them, e.g. "The multi-million naira contract for the supply of press equipment and modern computers to the Abia State Publishing Corporation may have been abandoned by the contracting firm after collecting a mobilization fee of over N100 million."

moin-moin /mɔi mɔi/ ground beans boiled to taste. Among the Igbo, it is known as mai-mai. (SL: Yoruba).

molue /molue/ Mercedes commuter township bus; mini passenger bus commonly used in Lagos, as in "Most molue buses have a capacity of about 100 passengers and they ply routes where poor commuters reside, especially on the outskirts of Lagos." (SL: Yoruba).

money-doubler one who dupes people of their money by promising them that he possesses the power to multiply their money.

monkey work, baboon chop a popular NE saying is "Monkey work, baboon chop", meaning "somebody reaping where he has not sown", e.g. "The successive military regimes in Nigeria have institutionalized a typical case of monkey work, baboon chop"; "The Yoruba leader made it clear that the continued practice of monkey work, baboon chop would not achieve true progress." This saying must have originated from the Nigerian Pidgin's popular saying "Monkey dey work baboon dey chop."

month-end refers to the end of the month, as in "I hope to settle all my debt by month-end."

moreso frequently used to mean "even more", e.g. "I am not in a position to offer you any financial assistance, moreso, my salary has not been paid."

more grease to your elbow! 'Grease' substitutes for 'power' in NE idiomatic expression "More grease to your elbow!" which is equivalent to BE "More power to your elbow!"—informally used to mean "May your efforts succeed!"

mosquito coil green material containing some insecticides. It is usually set on a thin metal holder and lit at the tip. Its slow burning produces smoke, which weakens and drives away mosquitoes.

motor park an open ground from where all kinds of vehicles are boarded and alighted, as in "See me off to the motor park." This is equivalent in certain respects to BE "bus stations".

mouth "mouth" is often used in NE idiomatic expressions such as: "Keep your mouth out of this matter" for "Don't interfere or be involved in this matter"; "Your mouth will put you into trouble" for

"You may be indicted by what you say"; "He's only making mouth" for "He is only being boastful"; "Don't put your mouth in this matter because you don't know anything about it" for "Don't interfere or say anything about a matter with which you are less familiar."

move with often used romantically with the meaning "associate with", as in "Johnny moves with only tall, beautiful women."

Mr. man a NE slang often used as a hostile way of addressing a man whose name is not known, as in "Mr. Man, complete your money or get down from this bus." It is also often used as a jocular way of addressing a familiar person, as in "Mr. Man, be fast so that we can get there in good time."

Mr. right often used to mean an ideal man for marriage, as in "Who is your Mr. Right?" There is also "Miss Right."

mudu /mudu/ measure for selling grain, e.g. "Is it why a mudu of garri goes for ninety naira instead of twenty naira?" (SL: Hausa).

mulatto people of mixed blood.

mummy frequently used as a polite form of address for a woman (usually older or of higher social status) who may not be one's mother, as in "Mummy, come and buy garri from me"; "Mummy, please dash me some money."

mumu /mumu/ idiot, e.g. "Why does he always allow

girls to cheat him? Anyway, he is a mumu." /SL: Yoruba).

my dear often used in NE by either sex to address either sex. In BE, it is not normally used by a male addressing another male.

my son popularly used by older people to address young persons, who may or may not be related. The question, "Don't you know that you are my son?" serves to explain to the addressee that he is distantly related to the questioner. "My son" can also be used by a completely unrelated person to a much younger person, as a strategy to attract sympathy, as in "My son, please help me." The same is also true of "my daughter". (Also in WAE).

N

NAFCON an acronym for National Fertilizer Company of Nigeria, a major fertilizer producing and distributing company based in Onne, Rivers State.

NADECO an acronym for National Democratic Coalition—a coalition of pro-democracy groups in Nigeria, as in "Most of the victims from the south are those employed during the tenure of the pioneer chairman of FRSC, Professor Wole Soyinka, labeled NADECO officers."

naira /naira/ the name for Nigerian currency. 100 kobo is equal to one naira, and about 140 naira is equal to US $1.

na lie! /nalai/ a loan-expression often used colloquially as an interjection. It may be loosely equivalent to BE "You are kidding!" or "You must be joking!" e.g.:
A: Have you heard that government has increased the salary of public servants?
B: Na lie! (SL: Pidgin).

naming ceremony a ceremony held some days after child-birth in which a name or names chosen by the parents of a newly born child is/are formally given. The events may or may not be preceded by an official religious ceremony.

NAN an acronym for News Agency of Nigeria.

national cake frequently used in NE to refer to commonwealth or federal government controlled revenue available for distribution among the states, local government areas and ethnic or regional groups, as in "He urged the Igbos to unite, especially in their pursuit for the national cake."

National Conference a conference of ethnic nationalities being demanded by civil rights' movements and some ethnic groups in Nigeria.

National Day Celebration also known as independence D cvay, the national day is celebrated on October 1 every year to mark Nigeria's attainment of independence from Britain, e.g. "The National Association of Nigeria Students (NANS) has threatened to disrupt this year's national day celebrations as it expressed support for the on-going strike by the Academic Staff Union of Universities (ASUU)."

national question often used to refer to the need for various ethnic nationalities in Nigeria to meet and discuss modalities for living together as Nigerians, e.g. "The national question is very important now, particularly in the face of ethnic-induced killings, which are regular occurrences in some parts of the country."

native often used at the lower educational level to mean "unsophisticated", "unrefined", e.g. "He is too native for my liking."

---

native doctor may mean a "herbalist", "soothsayer", or any of such healers using herbs, as in "The old man has been moved from the hospital to the house of a native doctor."

native music traditional music or folk songs.

na waao /na wao/ an expression of surprise or disappointment, e.g.:
A: Do you know that Gabriel duped his elder brother?
B: Na waao! I didn't know he could do that.(SL: Pidgin).

NDDC an abbreviation for Niger Delta Development Commission—a commission that is charged with the responsibility of providing social amenities for the oil-producing areas of Nigeria, e.g. "It is greatly bewildering and most saddening that the states of Anambra and Enugu are not included in the NDDC."

Ndigbo /ndigbo/ loanword for the "Igbo people", frequently found in NE, as in "The potentials of Ndigbo and indeed of all other ethnic nationalities in Nigeria have been stifled by prolonged military rule." (SL: Igbo).

NECON acronym for National Electoral Commission of Nigeria—body which was formerly in charge of conducting elections, as well as registering of parties.

NEPA an acronym for National Electric Power Authority. NEPA is often used in NE to mean electricity, as in "There is no NEPA in my village" for BE "There is no electricity in my village."

NEPU an acronym for Northern Element Progressive Union, one of Nigeria's political parties during the first republic.

never-do-well sometimes used in NE to describe opportunists and uneducated people who have suddenly made money through politics, fraud or other questionable means, as in "Politics is never attractive in Nigeria because it is dominated by the never-do-wells." In BE, this expression denotes someone who cannot prosper in life in anyway.

New Yam Festival the assortment of festivities that mark the eating of the new yam among the Igbo, as in "The New Yam Festival is the culmination of a work cycle and the beginning of another." In recent time, however, "New Yam Festival" has acquired various names among different communities in Igboland, such as "Ikeji festival", "Ahiajoku", "Iriji", or the marking of "day" in some communities, such as "Ihiteowerri Day", "Ihitenansa Day", etc.

news a clipped form commonly used to mean "news item" or "piece of information", as in "I have some news for you." It is also commonly used to mean "update" or "latest information", as in "Any news?" Some NE speakers often use an indefinite article before "news", e.g. "That is a good news." In BE, "news" is always treated as a non-count and is usually used as a singular noun.

next frequently used to precede a period of time, as in "I intend to visit my village in the next three months."

BE would use "in three months' time" instead of "in the next three months."

next tomorrow frequently used to mean the equivalent of BE "the day after tomorrow", as in "Abubakar will be going back to school next tomorrow."

next week often found in NE where BE would use "the following week", e.g. "He plans to travel next week" for BE "He plans to travel the following week."

ngwongwo /ngwɔngwɔ/ also known as "pepper soup", it is a rich dish of choice meat and/or fish prepared in a soup of hot spices; often served as an appetizer, e.g. "It is the practice in this community to visit ngwongwo joints every evening." (SL: Igbo).

NICON an acronym for National Insurance Cooperation of Nigeria.

Niger /naija/ derogatorily used for 'Nigeria', e.g. "Think of driving a stolen car and wearing stolen clothes. Niger for you."

Niger Delta the oil-producing areas of Rivers, Bayelsa and Delta states.

Nigerian factor a sobriquet for greasing the palms of government officials with mouth watering bribes to induce them into signing away large inflated state contracts, e.g. "The Italian marble dealer, Luttwak boasted of his familiarity with the Nigerian factor."

Nigerian English name for the variety of English used in Nigeria.

Nigerian Pidgin Nigerian Pidgin English—a 'contact English' commonly used in Nigerian cities and in ethnically heterogeneous communities.

NITEL acronym for Nigerian Telecommunications Limited.

Nkwo /nkwɔ/ fourth day of the four-day Igbo week; market that holds on Nkwo day. (SL: Igbo).

NNPC abbreviation for Nigerian National Petroleum Corporation.

no hanging a common inscription in commuter buses is "No hanging" meaning that nobody should stand at the door of the bus.

no more NE speakers frequently use this adverbial phrase where BE would prefer "no longer", as in "Our landlord is no more living here."

no noise may be equivalent to BE "Keep quiet." It is usually shouted by a somewhat respected person in an attempt to restore calm in a gathering.

no problem a response often heard when one is appreciated for a favour. It may be equivalent to BE "You're welcome" or "It's OK," e.g.
A: Thanks for the food.
B: No problem.

no standing usually printed or painted on the back of lorries as a warning to passengers carried by the lorries.

boli /bɔli/ roasted plantain. (SL: Yoruba).

---

nook and corner 'corner' substitutes for 'cranny' in NE idiomatic expression "every nook and corner" which is equivalent to BE "every nook and cranny", as in "We have searched every nook and corner of this room" for BE "We have searched every nook and cranny of this room", i.e. look or search everywhere.

noon in BE, this word usually refers to 12 o'clock, but some speakers of NE use the word "noon" to mean "the middle of the day."

North central one of the six geo-political zones of Nigeria, consisting of states in the northern Nigeria, such as Niger, Plateau, Nasarawa, Benue, Kogi, and Kwara.

North east one of the six geo-political zones of Nigeria, consisting of states in the northern Nigeria, such as Yobe, Bornu, Adamawa, Gombe, Bauchi, and Taraba.

North west one of the six geo-political zones of Nigeria, consisting of states in the northern Nigeria, such as Kaduna, Kano, Katsina, Jigawa, Sokoto, Zamfara, and Kebbi.

northern oligarchy frequently used as Nigeria's political idiom to refer to a clique in northern Nigeria that holds on to power in the country, e.g. "The northern oligarchy has condemned the call for the setting up of regional army, describing it as an invitation for secession."

not bad may be equivalent to BE "It is all right", as in:
A. How was your exam?
B. Not bad.

---

not quite long this adverb is used as an equivalent of BE "Not long afterwards", as in:
A: When did he leave?
B: Not quite long.

not so? frequently used in NE speech, especially, at the lower educational levels as a tag question which can be said to be equivalent to "isn't it?", e.g. "We agreed that you would return the book today. Not so?"

now pronounced with rising tone, it is a discourse particle (completely different in meaning from the Standard English 'now'—meaning at this time; at present), which is frequently added to the end of a clause in NE, either for emphasis, to attract sympathy or to make a command to sound subtle, as in: "Please help me now" (to emphasize a plea); "Go now" (to soften a command); "It is your turn to speak now" (an emphasis meant to serve as a reminder).

now-now colloquially used for emphasis, meaning "immediately" or "at once", as in "I want you to be here now-now." It may also be used to mean "a moment ago", as in "He just left my office now-now."

NPN an abbreviation for National Party of Nigeria, the ruling party during the second republic.

NPP an abbreviation for Nigerian Peoples' Party, one of Nigeria's political parties during the second republic.

NTA an abbreviation for Nigerian Television Authority.

Ntoo! /ntɔ:/ exclamation meaning "Serves you right!" "Told you so!"; mild rebuke for someone who ignored advice and has to face unpleasant results, e.g.:

A: Do you know that I was eventually duped of my money?

B: Ntoo! What did I tell you?

nwaada /nwa:da/ a title standing for "Miss", as in "Nwaada Grace Oji". (SL: Igbo).

nylon bag polythene bag.

nylon-tar a road that is smoothly surfaced with coal mixture laid on by a road-surfacing machine, as in "The contractor did a very nice job on that road, and I think it's a nylon-tar."

nze /nze/ a title for an ozo title holder, as in "Nze A. Okpara."

O

o! an interjection used to express excitement in a conversation, meaning 'What!' To a large extent, it shows the personal involvement of a participant in a friendly discussion.

Oba /ɔba/ "king", as in "The Oba of Lagos". It is also commonly used as a title usually prefixed to the names of the obas, e.g. "Oba Sijuwade", "Oba Adeyemi". (SL: Yoruba).

Obi /obi/ King; title for the traditional ruler of Onitsha, as in "Obi of Onitsha". Some traditional rulers in Igboland have also adopted the title "obi". "Obi" is also used to mean family house; main hall, as in "The Chief had to retire quickly to his obi because he was expecting some important guests." (SL: Igbo).

oburo /oburo/ the seeds of Aframomum melegueta; golden brown in colour and strongly aromatic, it is usually ground and used in soups, stews and sauces. (SL: Yoruba).

Obong /ɔbɔŋ/ title for the traditional ruler of Calabar, as in "Obong of Calabar." (SL: Efik).

Och /otʃi/ title for the traditional ruler of Idoma, as in "Och Idoma of Idoma."

odoziaku /odoziakʊ/ also known as "oriaku", it is a title for "Mrs.", as in "Odoziaku C. Okafor". (SL: Igbo).

Oduduwa /oduduwa/ "Oduduwa" is regarded as the progenitor of the Yoruba people. (SL: Yoruba).

odun /ɔdη/ a festival. (SL: Yoruba).

of 1. redundantly used after some words in NE in contexts where its use will not be found in BE. Some of the words are: "enough", e.g. "We don't have enough of spoons"; "less", e.g. "There is less of criminal cases in Lagos with the introduction of a special anti-crime squad known as Operation Sweep"; "much", e.g. "He has too much of problems already." In all these examples, "of" will be considered redundant in BE.
2. the preposition "of" substitutes for "with" in the NE expression "in company of somebody" which is equivalent to BE "in company with somebody", i.e. "together with somebody", e.g. "According to eye witness account, the late politician was seen in company of three strange men shortly before he was assassinated."

of recent analogical derivation patterned in the manner of "late" and "of late", commonly used to mean "of late", as in "Why haven't you been regular to school of recent?"; "According to him, given the political climate in the nation of recent, it was only fair that the next president come from the south for the benefit of the nation in its entirety." In both examples, BE would prefer "of late".

off a popular NE expression, especially, at the lower

level is "Please, off the light" for BE "Please turn off/ switch off the light"; "Off your trousers" for BE "Wear off your trousers. "Off" is rarely used as a verb in BE. BE would prefer to say "turn off" or "switch off the light." (Also in WAE).

off-head often used to mean "off-hand" or "from memory", as in "Some of our lecturers give their lectures off-head."

off-load frequently used in NE to mean "unload", e.g. "Please, off-load my goods. I don't intend to travel by this car any longer."

off-shore/on-shore dichotomy often found in the register of resource control, it refers to considerations based on territorial waters act as a reason to deprive states of oil resources that are found in their waters, e.g. "Ige may also, by taking the Southern governors to court over the off-shore/on-shore dichotomy, have incurred the wrath of Afenifere."

off spring often found with the plural -s in NE expression, e.g. "How many off springs does a pig usually have?" In BE, the form "off spring"—the children of a particular person, or the young of an animal—is never changed even for the plural.

officer 1. frequently used in NE to refer to a high ranking military personnel.
2. civilians often address uniformed personnel of whatever rank, such as police, the army, road safety corps, etc. as "officer", especially, as a way of getting

some favour, e.g. "Officer, please forgive the driver."
3. in the civil service, it denotes any highly placed
official, as in "The sole administrator has requested all
officers of levels 12 and above to attend the meeting."

ofo /ɔfɔ/ a symbol of authority represented by a short
carved stick; a refrain that expresses joint assent to a
particular course of action. It may also be a ritualistic
interjection representing "amen", as in:
A: May the gods protect us!
B: Ofo! (SL: Igbo).

OFR Officer of the Federal Republic—Nigeria's fifth
highest national honour, usually awarded to persons
who have distinguished themselves in their chosen
fields of endeavour.

oga /ɔga/ commonly used to mean "master" or "big
man", as in "Please, help me beg oga." (SL: Yoruba).

ogbanje /ɔgbandʒe/ mystery child believed to be
possessed by spirits, and likely to die young, and to re-
incarnate repeatedly to the torment of its mother; an
Igbo equivalent of Yoruba's "abiku", e.g. "I will not allow
things to continue this way, especially now you say they
have removed his ogbanje." In recent literature,
"ogbanje children" are referred to as "spirit children".
(SL: Igbo).

ogbeni /ogbeni/ the Yoruba equivalent of the Igbo
"Mazi", i.e. a title for "Mr." (SL: Yoruba).

ogboni /ogboni/ one of the major secret societies in
Nigeria, e.g. "An Anglican priest in Ogun State has

advised the members of Ogboni fraternity to renounce their membership of the society or leave the church." (SL: Yoruba).

ogbono /ɔgbɔnɔ/ species of the mango tree, the kernel of whose fruit is used in food preparation; the seed of the tree Irvingia gabonensis used in preparing soup, as in "Ogbono soup". Its fruit is also known as 'bitter mango'. (SL: Igbo).

Ogbuefi /ogbuefi/ a chieftaincy title. (SL: Igbo).

ogbunigwe /ogbuni:gwe/ a locally made bomb used by the Biafran soldiers during the Nigerian civil war, as in "When the CO arrived at that point he found Dansuku's men holding two rebel soldiers who were about to detonate an ogbunigwe." (SL: Igbo).

ogede /ogede/ plantain—ripe or unripe. It can also refer to banana. (SL: Yoruba).

ogene /ogene/ a musical instrument made of metal or iron, open at one end; also used by the town crier when he makes his rounds to proclaim an important announcement. (SL: Igbo).

ogi /ogi/ pap prepared from maize. It is prepared in hot water, and may be eaten with sugar, e.g. "Soon ogi was introduced into his diet, sometimes without powdered milk." (SL: Yoruba).

ogiri /ogiri/ castor seed; castor oil; spice made from castor seed; fermented oil-bean seeds of Parkia clappertonia, as in "Ogiri soup."

ogogoro /ogogoro/ locally distilled gin also known as kaikai, as in "The boat which had a capacity for 200 passengers, was loaded with jerry-cans of petrol and a local gin known as ogogoro." (SL: Yoruba).

Ogun /ogu/ deity, god of war and iron, e.g. "The local government chairmen and councilors should take their oath at the Ogun shrine." (SL: Yoruba).

ohaneze /ɔhaneze/ a pan-Igbo socio-cultural organization, as in "Ohaneze has condemned the use of public fund to finance rallies aimed at encouraging the present administration to succeed itself." It is sometimes referred to as "Ohaneze Ndi Igbo." (SL: Igbo).

ohoo! exclamation that expresses both surprise and disappointment. (SL: Igbo).

oil boom a period in the early '70s when Nigeria made much money from the sale of petroleum products.

oil money a constant reference to Nigeria's wealth which comes from oil, as in "His distaste for everything Nigerian, except the oil money, which enriches him by at least three million naira every month extends to the home game and the local players."

oja /ɔdʒa/ musical instrument made of wood. (SL: Igbo).

ojoro /odʒoro/ "deception" or "cheating", as in "Adamu is playing ojoro." (SL: Yoruba).

okada /ɔkada/ popularly used in some parts of the

country for "motor-cycle", commonly used in Nigeria for carrying passengers, as in "I don't like traveling by okada"; "Many retrenched workers have taken to okada transport." The name "Okada" is also usually called as a way of attracting the attention of a cyclist. (SL: Edo).

okada man motorcyclist, e.g. "The Okada man is stupid" for BE "The motorcyclist is stupid."

okay frequently used in NE where BE would use "I see" or "That's good", e.g.:
A. Have you got a job?
B. No, I intend to start a private business.
A. Okay. But, don't you think it will be better for you to pick a job in the civil service?
B. Okay.

okazi /ɔkazi/ vegetable with strong fibrous veins used to prepare soups and salads, e.g. "Okazi soup." (SL: Igbo).

okporoko /okporoko/ "stockfish"—a long strong cod and other similar fish cured by drying in the air without salt and believed to be imported from Scandinavian countries.

okro /ɔkrɔ/ the fruit of hibiscus esculentus used for thickening soup. It is a slim green pod, usually pointed, with slimy seeds and flesh, widely used as a vegetable in soups, as in "Okro soup." (SL: found in most Nigerian languages).

okwe /okwe/ large quick-growing tree of Riconodendron africanum whose dull white to brownish soft wood is

---

used for carving, and for paper pulp, the seed of its hard-shelled fruit serving as the tokens in 'okwe' game, e.g. "Sylva has been playing okwe since morning and has not attended to his business." (SL: Igbo).

Olodumare /olodumare/ "The Supreme Being", as in "At the dawn of time, when the world was in void and in chaos, Olodumare sent Oduduwa to the world with a handful of sand, a cockerel and the pantheon of Yoruba gods and goddesses as members of his entourage." (SL: Yoruba).

Olu /olu/ title for the traditional ruler of Warri, as in "Olu of Warri." (SL: Isoko / Urhobo).

Olubadan /olubadɔ/ title for the traditional ruler of Ibadan, as in "Olubadan of Ibadan." (SL: Yoruba).

Oluwa /oluwa/ "God". (SL: Yoruba).

OMATA an acronym for Onitsha Markets Amalgamated Traders Association, which is widely used in NE, particularly in the east as a derogatory term for "illiterate traders", e.g. "Even with his exposure in Europe, he is still reasoning like an omata"; "Blessing is married to an omata."

omo /omo/ "omo" is a popular brand of washing powder, but it is commonly extended to mean all brands of washing powder. For instance, when a buyer says "I want to buy omo", he may have in mind any brand of detergent or washing powder, such as omo, surf, elephant blue detergent, etc.

on a popular NE expression, especially at the lower level is "On the light" which means "Turn on the light" or "Switch on the light." BE does not use "on" as a verb. "On" is also used to form certain prepositional phrases not found in BE:

1. on admission. This is often used to describe a state of being admitted to the hospital, as in "His mother is on admission." This is equivalent to BE "His mother is admitted to the hospital."

2. on break. This is a coinage frequently used among the working class people to describe short break during working hours, as in "She is on break." Unlike NE, BE is usually specific on the kind of break—"unch-break", "tea-break", etc.

3. on seat. Frequently used as a coinage to mean "in the office", example:

A: Is the director on seat?

B: No, he is not on seat.

4. on table. Often used as a polite invitation to someone who arrives when one is eating, to join in eating the food, as in:

A: I am on table.

B: No, thank you.

5. on transfer. Frequently used to describe a state of "having been transferred", as in "He is on transfer to Abuja" or "He has gone on transfer to Abuja."

"On" substitutes for "in" in the NE expression "on the long/short run" which is equivalent to BE "in the long/short run", i.e. "with regard to the far/near future", as in "The increase in the price of petroleum products will have severe effects on the masses on the short run, but on the long run, the nation will be better for it." "On" also substitutes for "over" in the NE expression "speak on the phone" which is equivalent to BE "speak over the phone", e.g. "I spoke with him on the phone yesterday" for "I spoke with him over the phone yesterday."

on one's own accord   "on" replaces "of" in NE idiomatic expression "on one's own accord" which is equivalent to BE "of one's own accord", i.e. without being asked; willingly; freely, e.g. "They did the work on their own accord" for BE "They did the work of their own accord."

on top of one's voice   "on" replaces "at" in NE expression "on top of one's voice", which is equivalent to BE "at the top of one's voice", i.e. very loudly. E.g. "He often shouts on top of his voice" for BE "He often shouts at the top of his voice."

one   in BE, the pronoun "one" is followed by another "one" as a reference pronoun. In NE, "one" is often followed by "you" as a reference pronoun in the same sentence, e.g. "I keep on getting a lot of items that are sectional or promotional in nature in news-only-environment, yet when one reacts, you are not only reminded that this is a news-only-space but you are quickly called names." The use of "you" as a referring pronoun to "one" is unusual in BE.

one day is one day   a proverbial expression frequently used, especially at the lower educational level, as a threat suggesting that revenge or punishment is possible. It can be used as a simple sentence, as in "One day is one day" or as a kind of adjunct, as in "One day is one day, the thief will be caught."

one one naira frequently used in the context of buying and selling, and it is equivalent to "one Naira each" in BE, example:
A: How much do you sell your mangoes?
B: One one Naira.

only NE often uses "only" redundantly, as in "Give me just only one cup." BE speakers would prefer to use one of these two adverbs so that we can have "just one" or "only one".

onugbo /onugbo/ also known as "bitterleaf", it is a bitter vegetable used for making soup, as in "Onugbo soup." (SL: Igbo).

oo! an interjection that expresses acceptance. It may be equivalent to "yes".

Oodua an abridged form of Oduduwa (the progenitor of the Yoruba race).

OON Officer of the Order of the Niger—Nigeria's sixth highest national honour usually awarded to persons who have distinguished themselves in their chosen career.

Ooni /ɔ:ni/ title for the traditional ruler of Ife, as in "Ooni of Ife." (SL: Yoruba).

OPC abbreviation for "Oodua People's Congress", an

ethnic militia group; an association of militant pan Yoruba youths who claim to be fighting for injustice against Yoruba people, as in "An eye-witness said some youths believed to be OPC members and some ex-dockworkers' leaders stormed the Tin Can police station about 6.30am yesterday, chasing away the three policemen on duty."

open 1. commonly used at the lower educational level to mean "to turn on" (e.g. television, radio, tap, etc.), as in "Open the radio."
2. frequently used to refer to a party organized in celebration of the completion of a new house, as in "The chief is opening his new house today."
3. used idiomatically with the meaning "to get wiser", e.g. "I am not altogether a fool. My eyes are open."

open eyes become wiser; overcome timidity, e.g. "Nkechi has opened eyes now" for "Nkechi is now wiser than she used to be" or "Nkechi has overcome timidity."

open-handed frequently used as a NE idiom equivalent to BE "generous", as in "I like him because he is open-handed."

operated NE uses "to be operated" where the BE uses "to undergo an operation", e.g. "The footballer was operated on his right leg last week."

Operation Sweep a joint police and military venture which was successful in reducing Lagos notorious crime rate during the last military regime, as in "Marwa is retained in Lagos state probably as a result of the success of Operation Sweep in the state."

opinion tautological constructions involving the use of "opinion" and "think" or "believe" are more frequently found in NE than in BE, e.g. "In my opinion, I think you should resign"; "In my opinion, I believe he's not doing the right thing." In BE, only "In my opinion" or "I think"/I believe" would be more likely to be found and not both, within the same construction as the two sentences above.

opportuned "opportune" is used in BE as an adjective, as in "He arrived at an opportune moment." But in NE, it is commonly used as a verb to mean "opportunity" or "possibility", e.g. "Although he was a popular politician, he was not opportuned to make much money."

opposite some NE speakers use the preposition "to" after "opposite" in contexts where the preposition would be considered redundant in BE, e.g. "Our house is directly opposite to the bank" for BE "Our house is directly opposite the bank." In BE, when "opposite" is functioning as a preposition, as in the above sentence, "to" is not normally used.

opposition in NE but not in BE, this noun is often found pluralized, e.g. "The military junta has been facing a lot of oppositions following the hanging of a well-known playwright and environmentalist, Ken Saro-Wiwa." In BE, this noun is normally treated as a non-count and so does not occur in the plural form.

Oputa Panel human rights' investigation commission headed by a retired Chief Justice, Chukwudifu Oputa. The Oputa panel in Nigeria is akin to the Truth and Reconciliation Commission in South Africa. The Oputa panel was established to look into human rights' violation during the dark days of military dictatorship and possibly bring those that inflict excruciating pains and incalculable carnage on Nigerians to book. It also sets out to resolve past injustices and devastating agonies so that people can be reconciled, e.g. "Is Oputa panel a farce?"

ora /ɔra/ a vegetable (of the tree Pterocarpus; Canna indica L.) used in soup preparation, as in "Ora soup."

order in NE, the word "for" frequently occurs after the verb "order", but not in BE, as in "He has ordered for more drinks" or "The Inspector General of Police has ordered for the arrest of the students' union leaders." In BE, the use of "for" after the verb "order" will not occur.

oriaku /oriakʊ/ title for "Mrs.", as in "Oriaku Ifeoma Ibe." (SL: Igbo).

Orie /orie/ second day of the four-day Igbo week; market that holds on Orie day, as in "Most people in his community look forward to Orie market days because of commercial benefits associated with such days." (SL: Igbo).

original frequently used as a noun to refer to goods of superior quality, as in "Everything we sell in this shop is original." .

osu /osu/ Igbo caste system. (SL: Igbo).

Osun /ɔʃʊ/ river goddess worshipped in traditional Yoruba society. (SL: Yoruba).

other "the other" substitutes for "another" in the NE idiomatic expression "in one way or the other" which is equivalent to BE "in one way or another", meaning "by some means, method, etc.", e.g. "I must get a job this year in one way or the other" for "I must get a job this year in one way or another." In BE, "one way or the other" means "either way".

otokoto /otokoto/ a series of ritual killings in Owerri said to have been sponsored by the owner of the popular "Otokoto Hotel" in that city which later resulted in riots. All such ritual killings in Nigeria today are often referred to as "otokoto", as in "The two deputy Commissioners of Police successfully headed the State Criminal Investigation Department during the Otokoto killings."

our wife the phrase "our wife" is frequently used in NE as a reflection of the Nigerian world-view in which a wife is seen to be commonly owned, as in the question "How is our wife?" (Also in WAE).

ourselves there is the tendency for many speakers of NE to use reflexive and reciprocal pronouns together in a sentence, as in "We are meeting ourselves for the first time since ten years" for BE "We are meeting each other for the first time since ten years."

A: You didn't know that he too would face charges of coup plotting?
B: No, we were not allowed to see ourselves. I was in isolation.

out many NE speakers often insert this adverbial particle after some words in contexts where it will be considered redundant in BE, e.g. "leak", as in "The Minister is worried by the rate at which official information is leaked out to the public"; "lend", as in "I lent out the book to someone"; "spot", as in "I can't spot out the difference between the two." In all these examples, this adverbial particle will not occur in BE.

outside some NE speakers, especially the less educated ones often use the expression "to eat outside" as an equivalent of BE "to eat out", i.e. "to have a meal in a restaurant, etc. rather than at home", e.g. "She complained that her husband had been eating outside ever since he got a job"; "It is cheaper to cook than eating outside." "Outside" in this context may be interpreted by a BE speaker to mean "outside the house", "behind or in front of the house."

overload frequently used in the context of public transport to mean "excess number of passengers or goods", as in "I don't want to carry overload because of police."

overseas frequently used in NE as an equivalent of BE "abroad", as in "The man had just returned from overseas."

---

owambe /owambe/ parties and merry-making where people go and show off. It is usually associated with Yorubas, as in "Where were you the last time IBB came to Lagos for some owambe party?"; "Apart from the military, you abused the governors whom you accused of embarking on owambe foreign trips." (SL: Yoruba).

Owelle /owele/ a chieftaincy title among the Igbo people of Onitsha, as in the "Owelle of Onitsha." (SL: Igbo).

own 1. the particle' own' is often added in NE expression "Treat each case on its own merit" which is equivalent to BE "Treat each case on its merit", i.e. by or for its merit.
2. commonly used in the context of buying and selling, especially at the lower educational level, to determine quantity, example:
A: I want to buy some salt.
B: How much own?
A: Twenty Naira own.
"How much own?" will be equivalent to BE "For how much?" and "Twenty Naira own" will also be equivalent to BE "Twenty Naira worth." In BE, the determiner "own" is used after possessives to emphasize personal possession or responsibility, or individual character of something; belonging to oneself, ourselves, etc, as in "It was her own idea."

owner's corner in Nigeria, the owner of a car (particularly in a chauffeur-driven car) enjoys the privilege of sitting at the back right side of a car and this has come to be known as the "owner's corner" or "owner's side", as in "Don't sit at the owner's corner because Oga will soon join us."

oyinbo /ojinbo/ "white man". A popular NE collocation is "Oyinbo pepper", commonly used derogatorily to refer to the white man, e.g. "When some children saw Doctor in Port Harcourt, they thought he was a white man and started to call him oyinbo pepper." (SL: Yoruba).

ozo /ɔzɔ/ Igbo social rank, a title holder. (SL: Igbo).

P

pa used as a clipped form of papa, it is a respectful way of addressing the old, especially among the Yoruba and Bendelites. This title is usually followed by the person's surname, e.g. "Pa Awo", "Pa Rewane".

pack often used with the meaning "depart with one's property" with the new destination mentioned, as in "He has packed ı̸ another house." In this context, BE would prefer "move". On the other hand, the coinage "pack out" is its variant where no destination is mentioned, e.g. "The landlord has asked him to pack out before next Sunday."

painted with this preposition often follows "painted" in NE in contexts where it will not be used in BE, as in "His house is painted with a white colour" for BE "His house is painted white."

palaver "dispute", "quarrel", "problems", "trouble", commonly used particularly at the lower educational level, as in "Palaver is too much in this country" for BE "Problems are too many in this country"; "I don't want palaver" for BE "I don't want trouble." (SL: Pidgin, Portuguese).

palmfruit the fruit of palm tree from which palmoil is

made. It gets reddish-brown when ripe.

palmkernel the hard nut of palm-fruit which may be crushed and used in producing cosmetic oil.

palmoil red cooking oil from palm fruit.

palmwine a white-coloured fermented alcoholic drink from the palm tree. Among students and other young people, the slang "pammy" is often used as a clipped form of palm-wine.

pammy often used as slang, particularly by students to refer to palmwine, e.g. "Do you still have pammy?"

pampa /pampa/ slang for pre-prepared answers usually brought into the examination hall by students with intention to cheat, e.g. "The invigilation was poorly handled because many students who brought pampa into the examination hall were not caught."

panel-beat "to restructure", "to improve", or "to refine". This term was initially used in the context of restructuring the rusted body of used cars with the aim of improving their condition. But today, it is often used in other contexts with the same meaning, as in "I wonder if you will have time to go through this paper and panel-beat it for me so that I can get it published"; "Obetan assured that the bill had been panel-beaten, its over-riding provisions watered down."

pant many NE users use "pant" where BE speakers would say "pants" or "a pair of pants", i.e. underpants or knickers, e.g. "Where is my white pant?" for BE

"Where is a pair of my white pants?" In BE, this noun is always found in the plural.

papa same as "baba". It is often used as a respectful term for the elderly so that the person addressed as "papa" may not be one's biological father.

paper often used as an ellipsis for "a piece of paper", or "a sheet of paper", e.g. "Can you give me a paper?" In BE, this sentence will be "Can you give me a piece/sheet of paper?"

paper bag polythene bag.

parlour used as an equivalent of BE "sitting-room" or "lounge". On the average, a flat would contain 2 or 3 bedrooms, sometimes a dining and a living room, which is known as "parlour".

particulars frequently found in the context of police check points to refer to vehicle documents. A check is usually conducted to ascertain the validity of such vehicle documents, e.g. "Can I see your particulars?"

partner very frequently used in NE, especially at the lower level to mean "husband", "wife", or "fiancé", as in "He is my partner" for BE "He is my husband"; "She is my future partner" for BE "She is my fiancé."

passenger's side NE speakers often make distinctions between the passenger's side, the owner's side and the driver's side, in a motor car. The passenger's side is by the driver's seat in front of the car.

---

passport-size many speakers of NE often use it with a past tense suffix, e.g. "Each applicant should bring along photocopies of his credentials and two passport-sized photographs." In BE, "passport-size" functions as an adjective.

patience commonly used to collocate with "exercise", as in "The Minister asked us to exercise patience until the new budget is read." This collocation would sound too formal in an everyday context in BE, which would prefer "be patient".

pawpaw the subtropical fruit of the tree Carica papaya. It is usually round or oblong, of between 4 and 12 ins long, yellow when ripe, with a thin skin, sweet flesh, and numerous small black seeds grouped in its hollow inside. The leaves of pawpaw tree are often boiled and used in the treatment of cold or malaria.

pay this verb is often found in NE with the preposition "for" in contexts where the preposition will be redundant in BE, e.g. "He has paid for his school fees" for "He has paid his school fees." BE speakers "pay for" commodities but not for "fees"

pay before service this is a notice usually pasted in some restaurants and drinking houses requiring customers to pay before they are served their meals or drinks. A near-BE equivalent of "pay before service" will be "No credit sales."

PDP an abbreviation for People's Democratic Party, Nigeria's ruling party during the fourth republic.

pear in Nigeria, "pear" denotes the fruit of Pachylobus adulis which is different from the BE denotation of "pear" as the fruit of the tree Pyrus communis.

peg some NE speakers use the particle "down" after "peg" in contexts where most BE speakers would consider the particle to be redundant, e.g. "The only way to check inflation is for government to peg down the value of Naira."

pekere /kpekere/ fried slices of plantain (ripe or unripe) meant to be eaten. Commonly heard utterances in motor parks and along busy roads are "Buy pekere"; "Fine pekere." (SL: Yoruba).

pending some NE speakers use the preposition "on" after "pending" in contexts where it will be considered redundant in BE, e.g. "The union has suspended its strike pending on the outcome of this week's meeting with the university authorities." The use of "pending on" in NE may be in analogy with the use of "depending on."

people refers to persons, especially of a particular set or origin, e.g. "They are Ijesa people" for "They are from Ijesa."

PEP an acronym for Poverty Eradication Programme— a pet project of Olusegun Obasanjo's administration, which is aimed at reducing youth unemployment.

pepper soup meat prepared with much pepper in it. There are different kinds of pepper-soup—"chicken pepper-soup", "goat pepper-soup", "cow leg pepper-soup", etc. (Also in WAE).

percent often used as one word in NE, e.g. "Ninety percent of the world's rubber is currently produced in Asia, much of it in Malaysia." It is written as two separate words in BE.

perhaps may 'perhaps' sometimes collocates with 'may' in NE but not in BE, e.g. "This perhaps may be so" for BE "Perhaps this is so" or "This may be so."

perm sec a clipped form of permanent secretary, i.e. the head of a government parastatal or ministry, as in "Perm Sec lauds Indian film makers."

permanent frequently used in NE in the context of employment to mean "full-time" or "regular", as in "permanent job" for BE "full-time job" or "regular job", "permanent staff" for BE "full-time staff" or "regular staff."

person sometimes used in contexts where BE would prefer "nobody", e.g. "There is no person in the house."

personnel often used in the plural form, as in "All the senior officers and personnels of the armed forces are directed to take note of the development." This noun is never pluralized with -s in BE.

petrol station often used to mean "service station". While "petrol stations" known as "service stations" in Britain, offer car services, petrol stations in Nigeria rarely offer such services.

petty trader it is often used to describe someone who is engaged in small-scale trading with limited capital, e.g. "I don't really regard myself as a business man. I am only a petty trader." "Petty trader" may be equivalent to BE "small shopkeeper".

phone "to phone" is frequently used in Nigeria to mean "to give a call" or "to ring", e.g. "I have phoned you two times but you were not there" for BE "I have given you two calls but you were not there."

pick the particle "up" often follows "pick" in the NE idiomatic usage "pick up a quarrel (with somebody)" which is equivalent to BE "pick a quarrel (with somebody)", i.e. "to cause a quarrel with somebody deliberately, e.g. by behaving aggressively", as in "I don't know why she is always picking up quarrels with all her class-mates." The use of "up" would be considered redundant in BE in the sentence above.

pickin /pikin/ "small child", commonly used at the lower educational level, as in "I have not seen my pickin for a long time." (SL: Pidgin, Portuguese).

pick race commonly used among less educated NE speakers, and particularly in Pidgin English, to mean "run away" or "start running", as in "I thought we could confront the soldiers, but when they shot down two people, I had to pick race." (SL: Pidgin).

pick-up a small delivery truck or van, sometimes mounted with an iron frame to facilitate the transportation of goods.

pick up a quarrel "up" collocates with "pick" in NE expression "pick up a quarrel with someone" which is equivalent to BE "pick a quarrel with someone."

pin as a noun, it is commonly used as an equivalent of BE "needle" of a record-player. As a verb, it is often used with the particle "down" in a figurative expression where BE speakers would consider the particle redundant, e.g. "Chika pinned down all her hopes on her late uncle." BE speakers normally "pin their hopes on something" but not "pin down their hopes on something."

pineapple large edible fruit of the ground-plant Ananas comosus (Bromeliaceae).

pirate fraternity a secret cult popular within university campuses in Nigeria.

pitto /pito/ locally prepared beer such as burukutu. (SL: Hausa).

place in both formal and informal style, NE uses "place" for "house", "place of work" and "place of residence", e.g. "The meeting will be held in my place." The use of "place" in this context is very informal in BE.

plait commonly used to mean "weave", as in "She has promised to help me plait my hair tomorrow."

plantain the fruit of the tree of the family Musaceae which matures hard and with green skin. It is much larger than banana, and usually cooked as food. It turns yellow when ripe and usually fried and eaten with beans, rice, etc.

plantain-porridge porridge meal prepared by cutting unripe plantain into small pieces and cooked with some spices and other ingredients.

plate-number equivalent to "number-plate" in BE, as in "Since the introduction of the new plate-number, I have lost interest in memorizing plate-numbers" for BE "Since the introduction of the new number-plate, I have lost interest in memorizing number-plates."

play on one's intelligence idiomatically used to mean "deceive", as in "I have warned you to stop playing on my intelligence."

playing people deceiving people; lying, as in "Tyna is always playing people up and down" for Be "Tyna is very tricky" or "Tyna is very deceptive."

play-play colloquially used, especially among children to mean "a joke", as in "It was like play-play and before I knew what was happening, he had finished the food." (SL: Pidgin).

play the second fiddle the definite article "the" is often added in the NE idiom "play the second fiddle (to somebody/something)," which is equivalent to BE "play second fiddle (to somebody/something)", i.e. "to be treated as less important than another person, activity, etc", e.g. "Igbo leaders have decided never to play the second fiddle in the present political dispensation."

---

please a marker of respect often used where it is superfluous, e.g. "Can I please see you?"; "May I please talk to you?"; "Good afternoon please."

please kindly there is often the tautological use of 'please' and 'kindly' in NE but not in BE, e.g. "Please kindly help us" for BE "Please help us" or "Kindly help us."

plumpy "plumpy" is often used where BE uses "plump", as in "She now looks more plumpy than she was two months ago."

poff poff flour fried into balls and eaten as snacks, e.g. "All I am just trying to pass across is that the man should not just live by bread alone; after all, there is poff poff."

poke nose the idiom "poke nose" is often used as a NE equivalent of BE "poke one's nose into something", i.e. "to interfere in something that is not one's concern", as in "Why are you poke-nosing in this matter."

police this collective noun always takes the plural form of the verb in BE, e.g. "The police were immediately invited to the scene", but some speakers of NE use the singular form of the verb for "police", as in "We all know that the police is very corrupt."

political detainee a term that in Nigeria means prisoners arrested without charge, e.g. "He said that his government has released all political detainees." In BE, "Political detainee" would mean a person who is detained by police for political reasons, although "political prisoner" occurs more frequently than "political detainee."

politician frequently used to refer to anyone who can argue convincingly and persuasively without necessarily being in politics, as in "That man is a politician. He can present lies to appear as truth."

ponmo /kpɔmɔ/ a delicacy from cow skin, e.g. "The sale and consumption of a Nigerian delicacy, ponmo, in London has triggered the British Food Standards Agency (FSA) into an investigation on the illicit trade." (SL: Pidgin).

pool together "together" often follows the verb "pool" in contexts where it will not be found in BE, e.g. "He suggested that the three brothers should pool their resources together in order to build a hotel in their home town." In BE usage, "together" will be considered tautological since "togetherness" is already implied in the meaning of "pool".

possible-best there is the tendency to make redundant use of "possible" in NE expressions, such as "I have tried my possible-best for you" instead of the BE "I have tried my best for you."

postal the phrase "postal stamp" is sometimes found in NE where BE speakers would use "postage stamp", as in "Please enclose a self-addressed envelope plus two postal stamps of N5.00 each."

pot a frequently used idiomatic expression is "eat from the same pot," which suggests familiarity and the fact that people cook and eat together.

---

potato distinction is usually made between sweet potato (which is commonly grown locally) and Irish potato (which is either imported or produced in Jos-plateau areas).

poto-poto /pɔtɔpɔtɔ/ slippery clay that characterizes most Nigerian markets and untarred roads during the rainy season, as in "I try not to wear white trousers to Oshodi market because of poto-poto." (SL: Pidgin).

pound to beat up (somebody); batter, e.g. "When the armed robbers first came to our house, my husband was not around, and because they could not get much money, I was thoroughly pounded."

power-failure frequently used for "black-out", as in "We were unable to watch the world cup because of constant power-failure."

practicalize rarely used in BE, but often used in Nigeria in contexts where BE would use "put into practice", e.g. "The problem with Nigeria's education system is that we are always taught theories, and we never have the opportunity to practicalize what we have been learning."

praise often used in the plural form, as in "My people were full of praises for your kindness." In BE, this will normally be used in the singular form, "My people were full of praise for your kindness."

pray in NE usage, the preposition "to" often follows "pray", e.g. "He prayed to God for assistance and his prayer was answered." In BE, "to" does not follow the verb "pray".

PRC an abbreviation for the Provisional Ruling Council, the highest decision making body under military government in Nigeria. Also known as Armed Forces Ruling Council (AFRC), it is a "military parliament."

prefer some speakers of NE often use "prefer than" instead of "prefer to", as in "I prefer rice than beans" for BE "I prefer rice to beans."

prepare before I come when two persons have an appointment to do something or to go to somewhere together, one of them can warn the other against delays by saying "Please be prepared before I come" for "Please be ready before I return."

present a gift it is common to hear such expressions in NE as "present a gift", e.g. "The corper was presented with a gift during his send off party." BE usage would be specific on the gift presented.

presently commonly used in NE to mean "at present", "now" or "currently", as in "Presently, I am busy with my essay."

press commonly used in both formal and informal contexts to collocate with items of clothing where BE uses "iron", as in "I don't have the time these days to even press my cloths." However, "pressing" might be used in BE only in formal establishments such as hotels or in the register of drycleaners.

principal title for the head of a secondary school in Nigeria.

private school fee-paying school run by individuals in competition with public schools, as in "Despite the death of her husband, all her children still attend private schools in Lagos."

property commonly used in the plural form to refer to personal belongings, as in "The robbers came in the early hours of yesterday and removed all my properties." In the sense used above, this noun functions as a non-count in BE and therefore not pluralized. When it is found in the plural form in BE, it normally refers to real estate, land and buildings.

prostrate 'himself' is frequently omitted in NE expression "He prostrated before his father", which is equivalent to BE "He prostrated himself before his father", i.e. lying in a flat position, with the face to the ground as a show of respect.

public transport commonly used to mean "commercial transport", as in "Traveling by public transport seems cheaper these days."

pull someone's legs "leg" is sometimes pluralised in NE idiomatic expression "pull someone's legs" which is equivalent to BE "pull someone's leg", i.e. to make fun of a person in a playful way, as by laughing at some weakness or by making him believe something that is not true. E.g. "It's only a joke. I wanted to pull your legs" for BE "It's only a joke. I wanted to pull your leg."

pump a tap usually located within the house or yard, e.g. "What are you doing at the pump?"

pumpkin botanically known as Cucurbita pepo, its green vegetables are eaten as vegetable while its seeds are cooked and eaten. See also ugu.

pure water water (usually cold) packaged in nylon bags and sold in supermarkets, the road sides, in motor parks and markets. The collocation with "pure" does not suggest that the water is truly pure. It is common to hear women and children who hawk the water shouting "Buy pure water."

purse "purse" is metonymically used in both formal and informal style to refer to "money" or "funds", e.g. "It is the wish of my government to implement the new salary structure, but the purse of the state cannot accommodate such a huge bill for now." It is not used in modern BE in formal style.

put "put" sometimes substitutes for "take" in the NE idiomatic usage "put someone into consideration," which is equivalent to BE "take someone into consideration", i.e. "to make allowance for someone", e.g. "Whatever your plans, please put me into consideration." In BE, the idiomatic usage "take into consideration" is more likely to be found with reference to "something" rather than with "somebody", as in "I always take fuel consumption into consideration when buying a car."

put in the family way often used, especially at the lower educational level with the meaning "make somebody pregnant or to have a child out of wed-lock", as in "This was the man who put Angela in the family way and ruined her education."

put legs in one trouser a popular NE saying is "We will put our legs in one trouser" for "We will fight each other."

put mouth often used at the lower educational level as a NE idiomatic expression that means "to contribute to a discussion", as in "Please don't put mouth in a discussion which does not concern you." (SL: Pidgin).

put off "off" substitutes for "out" in the NE idiomatic usage "put something off" which is equivalent to BE "put something out", meaning "to extinguish something" or "to switch off", e.g. "Put off the candle" for BE "Put out the candle"; "Put off the light" for BE "Put out the light."

put on 1. commonly used in the register of clothing to also mean "wear", as in "I am putting on my new shirt." 2. frequently used for "switch on", as in "Put on the light", "Put on the radio."

put to bed colloquially used to mean "be delivered of a baby", e.g. "Hopefully, his wife will put to bed this week."

put up an appearance "up" replaces "in" in NE expression "put up an appearance," which is equivalent to BE "put in an appearance", i.e. to attend (a meeting, party, etc.) especially for a short time only. E.g. "I promise that I won't be long at the party; I only want to put up an appearance" for BE "I promise that I won't be long at the party; I only want to put in an appearance."

Q

quench /kwentʃ/ 1. used colloquially, especially among persons of the lower educational level, to collocate with "fire" and "light" for BE "put out" or "turn off", e.g. "Quench the fire"; "Quench the light." (SL: Pidgin). 2. often used as a slang in NE meaning "die", or "sudden cut off of engine", e.g. "Eat and quench" for BE "Eat and die"; "Quench the engine" for BE "Stop the engine."

queue "in the line" is redundantly used in collocation with "queue", e.g. "Queue up in the line" for "Join the line" or "Queue up."

quota system frequently used in NE to refer to a federal government system of reflecting all the ethnic groups and states in admission and appointment into federally-owned establishments, e.g. "He argued that afterall the southern peoples have in the past allowed quota system in some aspects of our national life where the north fairs poorly."

R

rabbit in Nigeria, "rabbit" refers to a giant rat of Cricetomys gambianus living in holes in the ground while the BE idea of rabbit refers to a gregarious herbivorour mammal of Oryctolagus Cuniculus.

raincoat a derogatory term for condom, e.g. "If you must have sex, always wear raincoat."

rainy season also known as wet season, it begins from March to October in the Southern Nigeria. (Also in WAE).

raise up the particle "up" often follows "raise" in contexts where it will not be found in BE, e.g. "That beautiful fence was raised up within one month." In BE, this particle would be considered redundant in the above sentence. "Boys, raise up your hands!" for BE "Boys, raise your hands!" or "Boys, lift up your hands."

rampant often used to mean "widespread" or "common", as in "Mercedes cars are rampant on Lagos roads these days." The use of "rampant" in BE has a negative connotation in that it denotes (especially of disease, crime, etc) existing or spreading everywhere in a way that cannot be controlled.

ranka ya dede /ranka ja dede/ also written "rankadede",

it is an address of praise to an older person by a younger one. It is also used as a blessing, meaning "May you live long." In recent time, this praise (usually accompanied by genuflection and the clinching of fists) is aimed at attracting some financial favour from the rich by the poor, as in "Perhaps, it is to constantly lubricate this rankadede culture, made more viscose by personal aggrandisement that informed the actions of some high ranking officials of the immediate past regimes to engage in a massive despoliation of the nation's treasury." (SL: Hausa).

rat while the BE usage distinguishes between "rat" and "mouse" mainly on the basis of size, this distinction is made in NE with the adjectives "small" and "big" rats, e.g. "A small rat had just run into the kitchen." "Mouse" is less commonly used than "small rat" in NE.

raze the particle "down" often follows the verb "raze" in NE constructions in contexts where it will not be found in BE, e.g. "In Ibadan, not less than ten buildings belonging to pro-Abacha campaigners were razed down completely." In BE, this particle will be considered redundant.

reach also used to mean "arrive" or "to get to", e.g. "He reached Abuja at 8.00 p.m." for BE "He arrived Abuja at 8.00 p.m."; "They reached their destination safely" instead of "They got to their destination safely." It is also often used without the mention of destination, e.g. "I have an interview in Lagos at 10 a.m., but with this bus I wonder if I can reach before the time."

reading in the context of higher education, a NE user asks "What are you reading?" for BE "What course are you pursuing?"

rear the particle "up" often follows the verb "rear" in contexts where it will not be found in BE, e.g. "I cannot even take care of myself how much more, rearing up a family at this time." In this sentence, "up" would be considered redundant in BE.

reason NE often permits the use of "reason" and "because" in the same sentence, as in "The reason why the new head of state released some detainees is because he wants the process of national reconciliation to begin immediately." The use of both "reason" and "because" in a sentence such as the one above will be found unusual in BE.

reassure this verb is often treated as intransitive in NE, as in "The leader of the government negotiating team reassured that the federal government will respond positively to your demands as soon as the strike is called off." In BE, the verb "reassure" is strongly transitive in that it is normally followed by a direct object.

receive used as a euphemism and a clipped form for "receive salary" in some sections of the country, especially among the lower income group, e.g.:
A: Have you received?
B: No, I have not received, but I heard that it will be ready tomorrow.

red-carded to receive red card in a football march, e.g.

"Celestin Babayaro was red-carded in the march against Australia." See also "yellow-carded."

red oil distinctions are usually made between palm oil which is red and vegetable oil which is not red, e.g. "While red oil is sold at N3,500.00 per 50 litres, vegetable oil is sold at N1,6000.00 per 20 litres."

refer back "back" often follows the verb "refer" in NE in contexts where it will not be found in BE, e.g. "Please refer back to the first paragraph of page two." The use of "back" will be considered tautological in BE since it is already implied in the meaning of "refer".

regard often pluralized in NE where BE will prefer the singular form, e.g. "With regards to your request, I will try to meet only part of it"; "I have very high regards for his wife." Although this noun is frequently pluralized in some contexts in BE, the singular form will, however, be preferred in the contexts mentioned above.

regret the use of the preposition "for" following "regret" is sometimes found in NE, especially, at the lower educational level, e.g. "He is now regretting for his action." The use of "for" after "regret" in this context would be considered superfluous in BE.

reject often used in the context of monetary transactions to mean "select", so that when a NE speaker says "These drivers are always rejecting money here", he intends to suggest that the drivers around him are being selective by refusing to accept dirty notes of money or some units of coins.

relax NE speakers usually ask their visitors to "relax" meaning "to feel at home", as in "Please relax, don't be in a hurry."

reoccur many speakers of NE use "reoccur" for "recur", as in "Military intervention is an incident that has been reoccurring in Nigeria since after independence."

repair shoes mend shoes, e.g. "You need to repair these shoes quickly" for BE "You need to mend this pair of shoes quickly."

repatriate in NE, "back" often follows "repatriate" in contexts where it will not occur in BE, as in "About 750 Nigerians residing in Britain were last weekend repatriated back to Nigeria." BE users will find the use of "back" in this sentence tautological since it is already implied in the meaning of "repatriate".

repeat again in NE, "again" often follows the verb "repeat" in contexts where it will not be found in BE, as in "Please, repeat again sir." The use of "again" in this sentence will be considered tautological in BE usage since "repeat" implies more than once.

reply the particle "back" sometimes follows reply in contexts where this particle will be considered superfluous in BE, e.g. "Thanks for replying back my letter immediately." The BE speaker will normally "reply to" a letter, and the particle "back" will be found unnecessary.

request for the NE speaker often uses the preposition "for" after "request", as in "He requested for a loan from the department." "Request" is normally followed by a direct object in BE and so the use of "for" would be considered unnecessary in this context. The BE user will prefer to say "He requested a loan from the department."

resource control a commonly used phrase in NE which is used in respect of the idea that states that produce resources should be allowed to control such resources and be made to pay some taxes to the Federal Government, e.g. "The Federal Government has been warned to handle the issue of resource control with utmost caution."

retiree refers to "one who has retired from work", as in "The introduction of the new pension scheme which was meant to relieve retirees of the problems earlier encountered at the Federal Ministry of Establishments has become a problem rather than a solution." There is no such word as "retiree" in BE. It must have been derived in NE in analogy with similar English forms.

return back the adverbial particle "back" is sometimes used after "return" in contexts where it will not occur in BE, e.g. "You should return it back if you no longer need it", "Hopefully, he will return back this evening." In BE, the adverbial particle "back" will be considered tautological in these sentences since "return" implies coming or going back to a place.

Reverend Father Catholic priests are frequently

referred to as "Reverend Fathers" in Nigeria, while they are simply "priests" in BE. "Reverend Father" also shortened to "Rev. Fr." is widely used as a title usually prefixed to the names of the priests, as in "Rev. Fr. Okonkwo", "Rev. Fr. Bamidele", etc. Similarly, "Reverend sister" and "Reverend mother" (also used as titles prefixed to names) are used where BE commonly uses "nuns".

reverse a popularly used expression in NE to suggest the thing that is contrary to or opposite of what has just been mentioned is "the reverse is the case", e.g. "With frightening adverts, one might think that young people would now be abandoning smoking, but the reverse is the case" for BE "With frightening adverts, one might think that young people would now be abandoning smoking, but exactly the reverse of this is true."

reverse back "back" is frequently used redundantly in collocation with "reverse", as in "Reverse back" where a BE user would pass on the same information simply with "Reverse" in the context of a backward movement of a car. The use of "back" will therefore be unnecessary in BE.

ripe-plantain the plantain that has become yellow-skinned and of sweetish texture. It may be cooked and eaten with stew, but very often, it is sliced and fried as a special side dish or menu item. (See dodo).

ritual killing also known as "ritual murder", it is the kind of killing of human beings often practised in Nigeria in which certain parts of the body of the murdered person are removed for ritual purposes, e.g. "Four people are currently being interrogated by police in connection with the recent ritual killings in the area."

River Niger name of an important Nigerian river.

roam the streets in NE, this collocation is commonly used both in formal and informal style to mean "move about", "move around" or "wander about", as in "The governor has authorized the principals to expel students who have cultivated the habit of roaming the streets during school hours." "Roaming" may be used in BE, but only in informal style.

roasted corn/maize distinctions are usually made between roasted maize and cooked maize, both of which are eaten as food or between meals.

robber bag polythene bag

rotational presidency in Nigeria's political idiom, "rotational presidency" is a phrase that is commonly used to refer to agitation that political power, especially the presidency should rotate among the six geo-political zones in the country, e.g. "The politician declared his support that rotational presidency should kick-off from the south."

RRS an abbreviation for Rapid Response Squad, an anti-crime outfit in Lagos state, e.g. "As the crisis raged, a team of Lagos state anti-crime outfit, RRS, was invited."

rub "rub" is a popular brand of cream used for the

---

treatment of cold or to relieve pain, but this meaning is usually extended to also include other brands of creams used for the same purpose.

rubber-slippers casual rubber sandals held on the foot by a v-shaped thong fitting between the toes.

rug often used as a verb, as in "I rugged my room for N8,000.00." "Rug" is used as a noun in BE for a thick, usually woolen, material that covers part of a floor.

running nose "to have a running nose" is an expression commonly used in NE to mean "to catch cold", e.g. "I have a running nose" for BE "I have caught cold."

running stomach "to have a running stomach" is an expression very commonly used in NE to refer to "dysentery" or "diarrhea", so that a sentence such as "Jane has running stomach" will be equivalent to BE "Jane is suffering from dysentery/diarrhea."

S

sabbatical leave the word "leave" often redundantly collocates with "sabbatical" in NE, as in "The professor is on sabbatical leave for one year." Since "leave" and "sabbatical" suggest a period of time in which one is away from one's job, the use of "leave" in the sentence above will be unlikely in BE.

sabo ngari /sabo ngari/ a settlement inhabited by people who are not of the same ethnic origin of a particular town. Also shortened to "sabo", it is commonly found in several cities in northern Nigeria where people from other ethnic groups and non-Muslims alike reside. Among some cities in western Nigeria, "sabo" is regarded as a settlement usually for Hausa Muslims. (SL: Hausa).

saaki /sa:ki/ a dress style that was in vogue at a time. (SL: Igbo).

safe journey greeting to one who is traveling.

salt the noun "salt" often substitutes for "insult" in the NE idiomatic expression "add salt to injury" which is equivalent to BE "add insult to injury", meaning "to make one's relationship with some people even worse by offending them as well as actually harming them", as in "Why should I pay these people a penny of my earnings? It will add salt to injury." The last sentence will in BE be "It will add insult to injury."

samba /samba/ a musical instrument in the form of a light weight leather drum, open at one end, with a flat wooden frame.

SAN an acronym for Senior Advocate of Nigeria, highest professional merit award for lawyers, which is equivalent to the "British Queens Counsel." It usually follows the names of these title holders, as in "Chief Rotimi Williams, SAN."

Sango /ʃango/ the Yoruba god of thunder and lightening, e.g. "Let the governors swear by Sango or Amadioha." (SL: Yoruba).

sanu /sanu/ a popular all-purpose greeting in northern Nigeria. (SL: Hausa).

SAP an acronym for Structural Adjustment Programme, e.g. "In a way, the devaluation of the Naira occasioned by SAP has contributed more than any single measure in destroying the moral fibre of Nigerians." It is often functionally converted from being an acronym to being used as a verb in NE, e.g. "This regime has so much sapped us that to eat is now a problem."

Sarduana /saduana/ title for a spiritual leader of the (Muslim) Hausa of northern Nigeria, as in "The Sarduana of Sokoto." (SL: Hausa).

Sarki /saraki/ title for a Hausa ruler of a small area or city, as in "The Sarkin Sasa of Ibadan"; "Sarkin Sudan of Wurno." (SL: Hausa).

satellite campuses distance learning programmes; outreach centres operated by many universities and other tertiary institutions in Nigeria, e.g. "The Executive Secretary of the National Universities' Commission has directed that all universities and other tertiary institutions operating satellite campuses should close down such campuses immediately."

satisfied used idiomatically in a sentence "I am satisfied"—a response commonly used in Nigeria after a meal, which is equivalent to BE "I have had enough."

says the time the question "What says your time?" is frequently asked in NE as a way of inquiring about time from someone who has a wrist watch or clock. This is equivalent to BE "What is the time?"

scale the verb "scale" often substitutes for "sail" in the NE expression "scale through" which is equivalent to BE "sail through (something)", i.e. "to pass an examination or a test without difficulty." This expression may have resulted from confusing the meanings of "scale" (i.e. "climb") and "sail through", e.g. "Thank God that I scaled through those difficult first semester examinations" for BE "Thank God that I sailed through those difficult first semester examinations."

scent vegetable a popular Nigerian vegetable with

strong aroma and taste which is used to prepare meat or yam pepper soup. It is also known as "nchoonwu" among the Igbo.

school often used as an intransitive verb in NE, as in "She is schooling in Enugu." BE would prefer the noun form, e.g., "She is at school in Enugu", or "She is going to school in Enugu." "Schooling" occurs in BE as a noun, meaning "the education one receives at school", e.g. "He has very little schooling."

SCID an acronym for State Criminal Investigation Department, as in "Seven persons were arrested and handed over to the SCID in Panti, Yaba, for further investigation."

scrape used, especially at the lower educational level, in the register of barbing or shaving to mean "shave off completely", as in "Scrape everything", that is, "Shave off the hair completely." The verb "scrape" (meaning "to move a sharp or hard implement across a surface, e.g. in order to clean it or remove something from it") occurs in BE, as in "scraping new potatoes." But it is not found in the register of barbing or shaving.

second often used by the less educated speakers of NE to mean "mate" or "companion". When a woman is asked "Where is your second?", it means that the husband of the woman is married to two wives the second of which is being asked after. But when a younger person, who is not married, is asked the same question, "second" here could be referring to a "roommate" or a "companion". This sense is absent in the BE meaning of "second" which among other meanings implies "next in time, order or importance."

second burial a traditional practice among some Nigerian ethnic groups whereby the funeral rites of the dead are more elaborately performed and celebrated. This is a follow up to the "first burial" in which the dead is hurriedly buried for lack of money or time. The "second burial" is, therefore, marked with heavier expenditure on food, drinks and other forms of entertainment, e.g. "His mother could give him no money because her brother's second burial ceremony had cleaned her out."

second day NE uses "the second day" where BE would prefer "on the following day" or "the next day", e.g. "He died and was buried on the second day" for BE "He died and was buried the next day."

securityman "watchman".

see this verb is often used in NE where BE would prefer "meet", e.g. "We have not seen since our graduation" for BE "We have not met since our graduation."

see me see trouble frequently heard as an expression of surprise that one is bothering oneself over a problem in which one is not concerned, e.g.
A: Why do you always wear a pair of shorts to the classroom?
B: See me see trouble.
This expression may be equivalent to BE "What concern is it of yours?" .

see pepper see red, as in "Leave her alone or you will see pepper."

see trouble get into trouble, e.g. "You will see trouble one day" for BE "You will soon get into trouble."

see you this expression is often used in NE as an ellipsis for BE "See you later."

self frequently used in Pidgin and colloquially by the less educated speakers of NE, as an intensifier that emphasizes a word or phrase preceding it. It may be loosely equivalent to "even" in BE, e.g. "There is no water self" for BE "There is even no water."

semovita "semovita" is a popular brand of "semolina", i.e. wheat flour used as "foo-foo", but it is commonly used in NE to mean all brands of semolina.

send-off also "send-off party", it is a party organized in honour of one who is traveling abroad or resigning from a job or on transfer to a different working environment. In BE, "a send-off" means seeing someone off to the place from where he will start a journey.

senior brother NE equivalent of "elder brother" in BE, e.g. "His senior brother is highly connected in government" for BE "His elder brother is highly connected in government." There is also the use of "senior sister" for BE "elder sister."

senior sister NE equivalent of "elder sister" in BE, e.g. "My senior sister will be getting married tomorrow."

---

for BE "My elder sister will be getting married tomorrow." See also senior brother.

senior wife refers to the eldest wife in a polygamous marriage.

service also "church service" , it is used to mean "church", e.g. "He has gone for morning service," equivalent to BE "He has gone for the morning section of the church; "Those of us who will not go for the revival should endeavour to attend the church service." BE would prefer "church" to both "service" and "church service".

serviceable in BE, this adjective means (a) "that can be used", e.g. "The tyres are worn but still serviceable"; (b) "suitable for ordinary use or hard wear", as in "serviceable clothes for children". Besides BE meanings, it can also mean "willing to serve", as is often heard in hotels and restaurants, e.g. "We are very serviceable." But when young men describe a girl as "very serviceable", it means that the girl is very loose.

settle 1. in BE "settle" may be used to mean "to pay what is owed", but in NE, it also means "to bribe someone", as in "The trouble started mid July when a police man shot dead a person at a road block over a disagreement on settlement."
2. popularly used among the Igbo in the register of trading. It describes an arrangement where a trader takes a younger person as an apprentice and sets him up in the same business after a specific duration of trade apprenticeship, e.g. "Some of us have served him for 8

years and he does not bother himself thinking about how to settle us."

3. the particle "down" is often used to collocate with "settle", e.g. "By now, you must have settled down for business in Kano"; "I have finally settled down in my new accommodation." The BE equivalent of the two sentences would be without the particle "down". In BE, "settle down to something" suggests that one has started to give one's attention to something, e.g. "Before you settle down to work, can I ask you a question?"

sha! /ʃa/ a discourse particle appended to a statement, which may be equivalent to "in short," in BE. It is very popularly used by young people as a style, e.g. "I will come, sha" for BE "In short, I will come." (SL: Yoruba).

shakabula /ʃakabula/ locally made gun, e.g. "Three months ago, the military administrator of Oyo State ordered security agents to round up all manufacturers of locally made double barrel guns otherwise known as shakabula." (SL: Yoruba).

shakara /ʃakara/ one who behaves "stylishly" or in a way to attract attention to oneself, as in "Don't make shakara for me." (SL: Pidgin).

shaki /ʃaki/ the lining of the stomach of a cow used as meat, popularly called "shaki" among the Yoruba. It is more generally known as "towel" in NE. (SL: Yoruba).

shape commonly used in contexts where BE would prefer "figure", e.g. "She has a fine shape" for BE "She has a fine figure"; "She has no shape" for BE "She hasn't got a very good figure."

sharap shut up! E.g. "Sharap your mouth" for BE "Shut up!" or "Shut up your mouth!" (SL: Pidgin).

sharia Islamic moral code. Nigeria's brand of sharia is seen by non-Muslims and people from the southern part of Nigeria as politically motivated, e.g. "What sharia are we talking about? Is it political sharia? If it is according to Muslim law, it is their right but they should not make it a political issue."(SL: Arabic).

shed also means "small shop" or even any space, especially in the market or by the side of the road where a trader sells some goods, e.g. "His business in fancy goods was profitable and his shed in Diobu market was one of the richest." "Shed" in BE denotes a small simple building, usually made of wood or metal, used for storing things or sheltering animals, vehicles, etc.

shekere /ʃekere/ a musical instrument in the form of calabash with a network of small black seeds on the outside. (SL: Yoruba).

shift frequently used in both formal and informal contexts in NE, e.g. "I will be shifting to my new house tomorrow"; "The concert has been shifted to the big auditorium." Users of BE would prefer "move" in the two contexts above. "Shift" seems to occur only in informal context in BE.

shining collocates with body, face, etc. in complimentary remarks, e.g. "Your face is shining" for BE "Your face looks very attractive,"; "Your body is shining" for BE "Your skin appears fresh" or "You are good looking."

shit as a noun, it means "faeces", as in "There is shit in front of the house." As a verb, it means "to pass faeces", as in "Let me go and shit."

shock an ellipsis for "cause an electric shock", as in "The electric iron shocked me." In the same context, BE would prefer "The electric iron gave me a shock", because the verb "shock" is an emotional rather than a physical shock.

shoe repairer cobbler, e.g. "The shoe-repairer is around" for BE "The cobbler is around."

shoe-shiner shoe-shine boy; one who moves around cleaning and polishing shoes for people for some money, as in "Call the shoe-shiner for me" for BE "Call the shoe-shine boy for me."

should in case the conditional markers "should" and "in case" are sometimes found together, especially in the language of the less educated speakers of NE, as in "Should in case you come before noon, do wait for me." BE speakers will consider the use of these two conditional markers in the same sentence as tautological.

show pepper punish; deal with, as in "I will show you pepper today" for BE "I will severely punish you today."

shunt a slang commonly heard among students who have queued up, meaning "to jump the queue", e.g.

"Shunting is not allowed."

side the use of "side" often occurs in contexts that are not found in BE, e.g.:
A: Have you been to Ikeja side before?
B: No, I have not been to that side before.
In the two sentences above, "side" would be unnecessary in BE, which would replace "side" with "Ikeja" in the second sentence.

sidon-look /sidɔn lʊk/ to keep silent; complacent, e.g. "The old politicians prefer the now famous sidon-look attitude to the current transition programme"; "He maintained a sidon-look attitude during the transition. programmes of both Generals Ibrahim Babangida and the late Sani Abacha." (SL: Pidgin).

sidon-lookers frequently used to refer to persons who exhibit the sidon-look attitude, as in "If anyone endangers the survival of our country as a nation, it is not those who call for a national conference. It is the complacent group, the sidon-lookers who oppose it."

since idiomatically used in NE as an adverb of time to mean "for a long time", e.g.:
A: When did you arrive?
B: Since.
The adverb "ago" is sometimes used redundantly in the same sentence with "since", as in "I have been in the village since two years ago." "Ago" will be unnecessary in BE in the above sentence.

sir used as a form of respect to an older man by a

younger person, and also to a superior by his subordinates. The use of "sir" in BE expresses formality as a form of address rather than respect, as exemplified by the relationship between the children and their male teacher in such statements in BE as "Please, sir, can I ask a question?"

sisi /sisi/ a clipped form of "sister" fondly used by the Yoruba for one who may not be one's own blood sister", e.g. "Sisi, how are you?"

sister 1. one addressed as a sister may be one's cousin, aunt, niece, or any female relation.
2. title of respect for older women by younger people, so that "Sister Joy" may be equivalent to "My elder sister, Joy." Sometimes, "sister" is used as a form of greeting or a way of attracting the attention of an unknown woman by a trader or by one seeking favour.

size 1. it is often used as a verb in relationship with wears to mean "fit", e.g. "This shirt does not size me. It is too small." In this context, it will be used as a noun in BE.
2. the noun "size" substitutes for "cloth" in the NE expression "Cut one's coat according to one's size" which is equivalent to BE "Cut one's coat according to one's cloth", i.e. "to do only what one can manage to do or has enough money to do and no more", e.g. "All the public servants who live far above their income have been advised to cut their coat according to their size."

sleep off commonly used in NE which may be equivalent to BE "fall asleep", as in "I was so tired that

I slept off" for BE "I was so tired that I fell asleep."

slippers NE speakers often say "slippers" where BE speakers would more likely say "a pair of slippers", i.e. "a pair of loose light soft shoes worn in the house", e.g. "Where is my slippers?" for "Where is my pair of slippers?"

slow-poison a dangerous person who pretends to be gentle, as in "He warned Nigerians not to be deceived by the gentle appearance of the former Head of State, claiming that he is a slow-poison."

slowly-slowly a reduplicative used colloquially in NE, particularly in the context of driving to denote an emphatic "slowly", e.g. "Driver, please stop over-speeding, go slowly-slowly."

small sometimes confused with "little", e.g. "Take the small boy along" for BE "Take the little boy along." Unlike in BE usage, "small" in NE is sometimes used to mean "small quantity of", as in "That money is too small for my needs." BE will use "too little" in this context.

small problem slight problem, e.g. "I have a small problem" for BE "I have a slight problem."

small-small a reduplicative used colloquially in NE to mean:
1. "small brand of...", as in "Do you have small-small beans?" for BE "Do you have small brand of beans?"
2. "little or gradual progress", in exchange of greetings, as in:

A: How is work?
B: We are trying small-small (for BE "We are making little progress").

small thing a commonly head collocation, especially among young people, meaning "Never mind"; "It doesn't matter", as in:
A: Thanks for your assistance.
B: Small thing.

snap in BE, the verb "snap" means "to take a quick photograph of somebody", e.g. "I snapped you in the beach." It is often used in NE to mean "to take a photograph of somebody", as in "Let us go and snap."

SMC an abbreviation for Supreme Military Council, Nigeria's military parliament.

SNC an abbreviation for Sovereign National Conference, a conference of ethnic nationalities, which is demanded by pro democracy groups, to discuss the national question.

so far "so far" is a NE version of BE "so far as", although they don't mean exactly the same. "So far as" has the meaning "as much as", "to the extent that" e.g. "So far as I know, the information is wrong", while "so far" has the meaning "provided that", e.g. "The examination is going to be easy so far you read your books."

soak-away a pit for sewage disposal.

social gathering a NE collocation which refers to a party or any gathering that attracts the presence of people, as in "The chairman directed that the hall will not be used for any social gathering until after the on-going renovation."

soft-drink non-alcoholic drink.

sokoto /ʃokoto/ men's garment of tunic and trousers, as in "The police tore and pulled out my traditional dress, agbada, and sokoto, leaving me only with buba and pants." It is also often spelt "shokoto", as in "He wore a shokoto to the place but found it torn to shreds after the mayhem." (SL: Hausa).

Sokoto caliphate popularly used in Nigeria's political context to refer to ruling Sokoto emirate and the northern ruling class which dominates political power in the country, e.g. "We ought to know if he is another instrument of the agenda of the Sokoto caliphate for perpetual domination."

solicit in NE, "for" frequently follows the verb "solicit" in contexts where it will not occur in BE, e.g. "This is not the right place to solicit for news." In this sentence, "for" will be considered redundant in BE.

Somehow 1. often used in NE as an intensifier to also mean "rather", e.g. "She is somehow tall." "Somehow" is used in BE as an indefinite adverb, to mean "in some way", "by some means."
2. strange; abnormal; unfair, e.g. "Your behaviour in recent time is somehow." for BE "Your behaviour in recent time is abnormal"; "The way you treated kate is somehow" for BE "The way you treated Kate is unfair."

something this indefinite pronoun is commonly used colloquially in NE to describe size, amount, or quantity which one is exactly not sure of. In such contexts where "something" is found in NE, BE speakers would likely use "about" or "plus" or "over", as in "He is paid twenty something thousand naira per month" for BE "He is paid over twenty thousand naira per month."

some times is often used in NE to mean "a considerable period of time", as in "I have not seen you for some times" where the speaker has in mind "a long time" or for "a considerable period of time."

sometimes this adverb is occasionally confused with some-time, as in "They plan to visit us sometimes next week" for BE "They plan to visit us some-time next week." "Sometimes" means "at times" while "some-time" means "at some uncertain or unstated time."

son of the soil a male indigene of a locality, especially one who is wealthy and/or influential, e.g. "When our reporter approached him for a chat, he obliged because he is a son of the soil." In BE, "son of the soil" denotes "one whose father worked on the land and who follows his father's occupation." (Also in WAE).

soonest Unlike in BE, "soonest" may be used in NE in a non-comparative basis, meaning "very soon" or "as soon as possible", e.g. "I am expecting your reply soonest" for BE "I am expecting your reply as soon as possible."

sorry it is more commonly used as an expression of

---

sympathy to one who has not been offended by one, for example, to someone who has just had a mishap or to one who sneezes. This sense of the word corresponds to similar terms in Nigerian languages. "Sorry" is used in BE to express an apology or a regret. NE speakers also use "sorry" to express an apology or a regret, but this sense is not as commonly heard as in the case of using it to express sympathy. (Also in WAE).

so so mostly; entirely, e.g. "The party was attended by so so men."

sound slang used mainly by young people to mean "music" so that "good sound" would mean "good music" rather than the quality of the musical production, as it will be understood in BE.

soup like BE, NE makes a distinction between "soup" and "stew". "Soup" in BE refers to liquid food made by cooking vegetables, meat, etc. in water, and usually taken as the first meal course. Similarly, "stew" in BE, is "a dish of meat, vegetables, etc. cooked slowly in liquid in a closed dish." In NE, the distinction between "soup" and "stew" lies on the content and the purpose for which they serve. The popular varieties of soup in Nigeria, depending on content, are "egusi soup", "vegetable soup", "okro soup", etc. Soup is used to eat "foo-foo" and "eba" or garri. On the other hand, "stew" primarily made of tomato is used for eating rice, yams, beans, potatoes, bread, etc.

source often used as a verb in NE, as in "We have five political parties, therefore, they should source their presidential candidates"; "The implication of the diversion was that the original intention for which the money was sourced was abandoned." "Source" is a noun in BE and is never used as a verb.

Southeast one of the six geo-political zones of Nigeria, consisting of states in the core Igbo areas, such as Abia, Anambra, Ebonyi, Enugu and Imo.

Southsouth one of the six geo-political divisions of Nigeria, consisting of states in the Southern minority groups such as Akwa Ibom, Bayelsa, Cross Rivers, Delta, Edo and Rivers.

Southwest one of the six geo-political zones of Nigeria, consisting of states in the core Yoruba areas, such as Ekiti, Lagos, Ogun, Ondo, Osun and Oyo.

spare ellipsis for "spare tyre", commonly used by commercial drivers, as in "Help me with your spare."

speak with two mouths an idiomatic expression popularly used among the Igbo, referring to a state of dishonesty or unreliability, e.g. "He doesn't speak with two mouths. When he said yes, it is yes" for BE "He is very honest and reliable."

spirit money also known as spiritual money, it is frequently used to refer to amazing wealth made through spiritual invocation of money, e.g. "Come to us for success, progress and spiritual money invocation"; "It is generally believed that people indulge in ritual killings for spirit money."

spiritual leader leader of a spiritual church in Nigeria, such as Celestial Church of Christ, Eternal Sacred Order of Cherubim and Seraphim, etc.

spoil often used to collocate with nouns denoting pieces of equipment or items of technology, where BE would prefer to use "out of order", e.g. "My radio is spoilt" for BE "My radio is out of order."

sponsor also used in NE in contexts where BE would prefer "benefactor", as in the payment of school fees, in marriage, etc., e.g. "My sponsor threatened to stop paying my fees if I continue to be a member of secret cult"; "The wedding was delayed because of the inability of our sponsors to arrive at the church early."

spray frequently used to collocate with "money" or "Naira" with the meaning "give money openly as a way of showing admiration." Money (usually currency notes) is often "sprayed" to musicians or dancers in parties such as weddings, burials, naming ceremony, etc., as a gesture of encouragement, admiration, and also for acknowledgment and publicity, e.g. "The performance of Sunny Ade was so impressive that even other musicians joined in spraying him with money." In BE, "spray" is understood in the sense of "a liquid sent through the air in tiny drops, e.g. by the wind or through an apparatus."

staff "a staff" is often used as an ellipsis for "a member of staff", e.g. "We now have a new staff." Although "a staff" in place of "a member of staff" is sometimes heard in contemporary BE, the usage is more frequently used in NE than in BE.

stalites frequently found in the register of higher educational institutions to refer to old students, as in "Orlu Zonal Students' Association welcomes all students, both freshers and stalites to the campus."

starch food prepared by filtering ground cassava and steering it in hot water, popular in Delta state.

starts from sometimes heard in NE with the meaning "starts on", e.g. "Our second semester examination starts from Monday" for BE "Our second semester examination starts on Monday."

state police some states are agitating that states be allowed to control police in Nigeria rather than the present practice in which the Nigeria Police Force is entirely under the control of Federal Government, e.g. "There are other things outside resource control like state police."

station frequently used to refer to one's place of work or the location of one's official duties, e.g. "I will not be in my station for two weeks"; "I hope they don't sack me because I have been out of station for too long." The use of "station" as exemplified in these two sentences is not found in BE. (Also in WAE).

stay "to stay" (with someone) is often used to also mean "to live" (with someone), as in "Adamu has been staying with Amfani in Lagos for the past three years." A BE speaker would prefer to say "Adamu has been living with Amfani for the past three years."

steering frequently used as an ellipsis for "steering wheel" of a vehicle, as in "My steering is bad" for BE "My steering wheel is bad." (Also in WAE).

step "step" often substitutes for "tread" in the NE idiomatic expression "step on somebody's toes" which is equivalent to BE "tread on somebody's toes", i.e. "to offend or annoy somebody", e.g. "I don't want to step on anybody's toes" for BE "I don't want to tread on anybody's toes."

step aside equivalent to BE "step down." When "step aside" is used in NE, it is interpreted to mean "to wait for a convenient opportunity to step in again."

sticks ellipsis for "sticks of cigarette", e.g. "Give me two sticks" for BE "Give me two sticks of cigarette."

still yet many speakers of NE use "still yet" where BE uses either "still" or "yet", e.g. "Her husband provides all her needs, still yet she runs after men."

stockfish a special brand of dried fish believed to be imported from Scandinavian countries, e.g. "I found the store already filled with food: stockfish, yams, garri, oil." See also "okporoko".

stomach is coming out a commonly used expression of compliment in NE is "Your stomach is coming out" for BE "Your stomach is protruding." Protruding stomach in Nigeria suggests evidence of good living or improved condition of living.

stomach pain stomach ache or upset, as in "I have

stomach pain" for BE "I feel a serious stomach upset" or "I am experiencing severe stomach ache."

storey building in NE, "storey building" is a building with several floors or storeys and is therefore the opposite of "bungalow", e.g. "He has two storey buildings in Onitsha."

stranger 1. often used to also mean a "guest" or "visitor". "Stranger" ought to mean a person who is not familiar to one, but in Nigeria, even one's closest friend still considers himself to be a stranger in his friend's house as long as he does not live there, e.g.:
A: Please my wife does not allow strangers into her kitchen.
B: Look John, as your younger brother, I don't consider myself as a stranger in your house.
2. in Nigeria, even in a city where one was born and has lived all one's life, one still thinks of oneself as a "stranger" as long as that city is not ones "home-town."

strangle the phrase "to death" is often used to collocate redundantly with "strangle", as in "The pilot was strangled to death by her domestic staff." In the context used above, a BE user will find the phrase "to death" redundant.

stress as in many non-native varieties of English, "on" is used after this verb in contexts where it will not be found in BE, e.g. "The Vice Chancellor stressed on their need for parents to monitor closely the activities of the children to prevent them from negative influences." "On" would be considered unnecessary by the speakers of BE in the sentence given above.

stretcher out "stretcher" is a noun in BE, meaning "a framework of poles with a long piece of canvas attached between them, used for carrying a sick or injured person." In NE, it is sometimes inflected for past tense, as in "She injured herself during training and was stretchered out" for BE "She injured herself during training and was carried out on a stretcher"; "Late in the second half, two Ghanaians were injured and were stretchered out."

strong "strong" is preferred to "tough" in certain contexts where the meaning is "hard to break or cut", as in "This meat is too strong" for BE "This meat is too tough."

stronghead stubborn; obstinacy, as in "Andrew is a nice man. His only problem is stronghead"; "Ikenna is fond of proving strong head" for BE "Ikenna is stubborn."

student in NE usage, a "student" is anyone studying in an educational institution above primary school level. In BE, "student" denotes someone studying in a higher institution. Thus the NE "secondary school student" is equivalent to BE "secondary school pupil."

substitute the preposition "with" sometimes follows the verb "substitute" in NE where BE will use "for", as in "His name was substituted with that of Lt. Maina, a nephew to the then Brig. Abacha who was less qualified for the sponsorship." In this sentence, a BE speaker will certainly use "for" and not "with" after "substitute".

succeed often used in NE to collocate with "with" instead of with "in", as in "God will help all of us to succeed with our studies" for BE "God will help all of us to succeed in our studies."

suffer used in NE to also mean "cause suffering to", e.g. "She really suffered me before I married her."

suffer-head mostly used in Pidgin and in NE by the less educated people to mean "a luckless person", e.g. "I don't blame him for giving me all his work to type for him. He has seen a suffer-head."

sugar cane cane-like stem with hard covering, containing sugar-taste liquid.

sugar-daddy a promiscuous old man who is having sexual affairs with women as young as his own daughters, usually in exchange for money or material acquisition, e.g. "Bimpe`s sugar-daddy bought a brand new Toyota car for her." (Also in WAE).

Sultan /sɔltan/ title for the head of the Sokoto Caliphate who is also the spiritual leader for Nigerian Muslims, as in "The Sultan of Sokoto." (Arabic).

sunshades a NE equivalent of "sunglasses" in BE. "Sunshade" in BE denotes some other forms of protection such as a parasol.

Super Eagles name for Nigeria's senior national football team.

suppose many speakers of NE tend to use "suppose" where they ought to use "supposed", e.g. "We are suppose to be on the side of the people not on the side of the oppressor." "Supposed" rather than "suppose" would be used in this context in BE.

supposing like in many non-native varieties of English, the use of double conjunctions often occur in NE, as in "Supposing if he dies tomorrow, what will happen to the poor children?" In this example speakers of BE would use either "supposing" or "if" but not the two together as used above.

sure banker meaning "certainty". It started as coinage used within schools to refer to questions that are most likely to be asked in examinations, but it is today used in other contexts for "certain", i.e. "sure beyond doubt", as in "His coming back today is a sure banker" for BE "His coming back is certain."

surety sometimes used, especially at the lower educational level, as a verb, e.g. "Even his own brother refused to surety for him." "Surety" is always a noun in BE and so the above sentence will be "Even his own brother refused to act as a surety for him."

surplus often used, especially, at the lower educational level to mean "very much" or "very many", e.g. "Mercedes cars are surplus in Lagos", but the intention here is to suggest that "There are many Mercedes cars in Lagos." In BE, "surplus" means "more than required" or "in excess".

suspend the topic frequently used in both formal and informal styles in NE to mean "Stop what one was saying", as in "Let us suspend this gist until later." In BE, "suspend" would be used only in formal style.

sustain an injury frequently used in both formal and informal styles in NE, e.g. "He sustained a little injury as a result of the accident." This collocation might occur in formal style in BE but not in everyday usage.

suya /sʊja/ roasted meat with a lot of spices. (Also in WAE, SL: Hausa).

swallow often used in the context of eating in the sense not found in BE. This follows the fact that certain food such as foo-foo, amala, tuwo, etc. are swallowed without chewing, e.g. "Do you know that some people cannot swallow eba without chewing it?" In BE, every food is chewed before being swallowed.

sweet 1. frequently used to mean "tasty" or "delicious", as in "The soup is very sweet"; "Buy sweet food." In BE, edible things are described as "sweet" if they taste like sugar.
2. sometimes used to mean "interesting", as in "The film was very sweet" for BE "The film was very interesting."

sweet mouth flattering, friendly, deceptive talk intended to persuade someone or to pacify people, as in "Nigerian politicians always use sweet mouth to deceive the people."

---

sweet potato a sweetish, edible tuber with a purple or pinkish skin and cream or grey flesh. It is a root-crop, smaller than yam tuber.

T

taa! /taː/ interjection suggesting that the speaker should immediately stop an on-going discussion, as in:
A: Would you like to be my girlfriend?
B: Taa! (SL: Igbo).

tailor in BE, a "tailor" is one who makes men's clothes. In NE, a "tailor" is anybody who makes clothes—both men's clothes and women's dresses.

take as in some non-native varieties of English, NE speakers often use this verb in contexts where BE would select different verbs. Examples include: "He took permission from his head of department" (obtained); "Let me go and take my bag" (fetch or get); "I take only mineral" (drink); "He takes a lot of pepper" (eats); "He doesn't take food before going to school" (have); "Did the university take you?" (admit). NE also uses the collocation "to take the light" for BE "To make a power cut", e.g. "Our light has been taken" for BE "Our power has been caught." "Take" often collocates with food, lunch, breakfast, bath, etc., e.g. "I took my lunch at 3 o' clock" for BE "I had my lunch at 3 o' clock"; "Go and take your bath" for BE "Go to have your bath."

take in a NE idiom meaning "to become pregnant", as in "I asked her to stop her job because she had just taken in" for BE "I asked her to stop her job because she had

---

just become pregnant."

take light seize power, as in "NEPA has taken the light again" for BE "NEPA has seized power supply again."

take picture a NE equivalent of "to pose for a photograph", e.g. "My sister has gone to take picture" for BE "My sister has gone to pose for a photograph"; "Come and take us picture" for BE "Come and take a photograph of us."

take time an idiomatic expression with the meaning "Be careful", and often used in the imperative mood as a warning, e.g. "Take time! I am warning you for the last time." "Take one's time" is a BE idiom with the meaning "not to hurry." The expression, "That will take time" denotes that it cannot be done quickly.

talakawa /talakawa/ "the masses" or "the poor commoners", as in "He told us that they, the talakawas, have been fighting this group for decades now." (SL: Hausa).

talk less a connective commonly used in NE as an equivalent of BE "let alone", as in "He doesn't have a bicycle, talk less of a car"; "I cannot feed myself, talk less of feeding a woman." In both examples, a BE user would prefer "let alone."

talk true! a popular NE expression, especially at the lower educational level, meaning "Are you serious?", "Be serious!", as in:
A: Our director has been retired.
B: Talk true!

talking lie lying or telling a lie, e.g. "He is talking lie" for BE "He is lying" or "He is telling a lie."

talking terms "talking" substitutes for "speaking" in the NE idiomatic expression "be on talking terms" which is equivalent to BE "be on speaking terms", meaning "to be on friendly or polite terms; to be willing to talk to somebody, especially after an argument", e.g. "He has not been on talking terms with his elder brother after the disagreement over their father's will" for BE "He has not been on speaking terms with his elder brother after the disagreement over their father's will."

tangerine a species of orange that is smaller in size and with slightly different taste.

tape ellipsis for "tape-recorder" or "radio-cassette", e.g. "Can you allow me to use your tape for a party?" for BE "Can you allow me to use your tape-recorder for a party?"

taper an ellipsis for "rubber taper" or "palm wine taper", i.e. one who taps rubber or palm trees, as in "Austin is now a taper" for "Austin is now a rubber/ palm wine taper."

tap-water also pump-water, i.e. any water drawn from tap that is supplied by the Water Works department. It denotes water of good quality, different from rain-water, well-water, stream-water, etc.

taste the word "taste" substitutes for "proof" in the NE idiomatic expression "The taste of the pudding is in the eating" which is equivalent to BE "The proof of

---

the pudding is in the eating", meaning "the real value of somebody or something can be judged only from practical experience and not from appearance or theory."

tatashi /tataʃi/ a species of fresh pepper, usually longer than normal pepper and less hotter. It serves to make soup or stew very reddish and therefore very attractive. (SL: Hausa).

taxi park a large area set aside for the loading and the off-loading of taxis only.

tea "tea" in Nigeria refers to any beverage with a hot water base, although it can sometimes be taken in cold water. "Tea" in NE usage would therefore include drinks made from tea bags, coffee, and chocolate drinks such as Bournvita, Ovaltine, Milo, etc. "Tea" in BE usage is essentially made of tea leaves or tea bags.

tear this is a NE equivalent of BE "tear up", e.g. "You can tear the paper if you like" for BE "You can tear up the paper if you like."

ten per cent in NE, "ten per cent" describes corrupt practices among government officials in which any contract award or supply attracts a ten per cent bribe which the government official collects before signing the contract, e.g. "The former military governor made sure he collected ten per cent of all contracts signed before leaving office."

than sometimes used where BE would prefer "rather than", e.g. "Members of the union are prepared to lose their jobs than call off the strike"; "I prefer rice than beans." BE would use "rather than" in the first sentence and "to" in the second sentence.

thank God idiomatic usage; a popular NE response "We thank God" in exchange of greetings may loosely be equivalent to BE "fine", e.g.:
A: How is work?
B: We thank God.
However, in the next context, "We thank God" would be equivalent to "They are well" in BE.
A: How is your family?
B: We thank God.

thanks the greeting "Thanks for yesterday" is commonly used in Nigeria for favour done the previous day.

the hand writing on the wall 'hand' is often added in the NE idiomatic expression "the hand writing on the wall" which is equivalent to BE "the writing on the wall", meaning clear signs that warn of failure, disaster or defeat, as in "Many see these pit closures as the hand writing on the wall for the whole mining industry" for BE "Many see these pit closures as the writing on the wall for the whole mining industry."

their own often used for "theirs", e.g. "The table and chair belong to us, but I think the fan is their own" for BE "The table and chair belong to us, but I think the fan is theirs."

themselves commonly used to refer to "each other" or "one another", e.g. "Joy and Chike met themselves yesterday after fifteen years"; "At the end of the football match, players from the two teams embraced themselves in the spirit of sportsmanship." BE usage would prefer "each other" and "one another", respectively, for the two sentences above.

these frequently used in NE as an anaphoric pronoun referring to several abstract entities, where BE uses "this", e.g. "He buys clothes for me, he gives me money for housekeeping, he has installed electricity and television. I thank him for all these." In this sentence, "this" rather than "these" would be acceptable in BE.

thick madam slang for "a wealthy woman", e.g. "Oga's wife is a thick madam."

this your the use of double pronouns is sometimes found in NE expressions, as in "This your friend is not reliable" for BE "This friend of yours is not reliable" or "Your friend is not reliable."

those days a commonly used phrase in NE "in those days" is equivalent to BE "in the past", e.g. "Mallam Abubakar used to be rough in those days" for BE "Mallam Abubakar used to be rough in the past."

though many speakers of NE often use double conjunction constructions such as "Though the man was poor but he was able to give university education to his children." BE usage would accept either of the two but not both of them in the example above.

tight difficult, e.g. "Things are very tight for me" for BE "I am in a very difficult financial situation."

tight friend NE uses this collocation to mean "close friend" or "bosom friend", as in "Babangida and Abacha are tight friends."

till the use of "till" in NE often leads to different interpretation of meaning from BE, e.g. "The book has not been found till today." This sentence is not very likely to occur in BE, and where it does, it would be interpreted by a BE speaker to mean that the missing book has been found today. A NE user of this construction intended to convey the meaning that the book is still missing. A BE equivalent of this sentence would be "The book has still not been found."

till then frequently used in formal greetings as an equivalent of BE "See you later."

till tomorrow a popular NE greeting which is equivalent to BE "good night."

time 1. a commonly used NE idiomatic expression, "Time is against me/us" may be equivalent to BE "I/ We haven't got much time."
2. "missing her time" in NE suggests the absence of menstruation, as in "Doctor, I suspect she is pregnant because she has been missing her time for the past two months."

tin-cutter this word is used for BE "tin-opener".

tiny often used in description of persons where BE would prefer "thin" or "skinny", e.g. "Her legs are tiny" for BE "Her legs are thin."

---

tipper an ellipsis for "tipper lorry" or "tipper trunk", i.e. a lorry with a large container at the back which can be raised at one end to tip out the content, usually sand, e.g. "He bought a tipper" for "He bought a tipper lorry."

titi /titi/ "young woman", as in "Titi, get me some drinking water." It may also mean pretty girl, as in "There are many titis in this town" for BE "There are many pretty girls in this town." (SL: Yoruba).

to the "to infinitive" constructions after nouns occur frequently in NE where BE would prefer gerund, as in "Instead of reading his books, he wastes much of his time to visit his irresponsible friends" for BE "Instead of reading his books, he wastes much of his time visiting his irresponsible friends."

to and fro also used in the context of journeys to mean "return", as in "You have to budget at least N2000.00 for the journey, to and fro." In such contexts, "return" is hardly used in NE unlike in BE, but instead "going and coming back" and "to and fro" are used with the same meaning.

to see often used especially among corrupt government officials in the sense of offering bribe, e.g. "You have to see Inspector" for "You have to give Inspector some bribe."

tokunbo /tokwunbɔ/ second hand goods, especially imported used cars, electronics and machinery, e.g. "The prices of tokunbo cars have fallen by 30% following the liberalization of import regulations in the 1998 budget." (SL: Yoruba).

---

tombo liquor   often used particularly by students for palmwine, as in "He has gone to bring some bottles of tombo liquor." 'Tombo' is sometimes used as the elliptic form of 'tombo liquor'.

tongue is too sharp   talkative, e.g. "Your tongue is too sharp" for BE "You are a talkative."

too-know   commonly used in NE, especially at the lower educational level where BE would use "bragging", e.g. "The problem with young people of today is simply too-know. They don't always believe that somebody knows more than they do."

too much/many   often used for "Much/many", as in "We have too many millionaires in Nigeria today" where the context suggests "many". Similarly, many NE users use "too" with the meaning "very", as in "Meat was too cheap in the market yesterday" for BE "Meat was very cheap in the market yesterday"; "The sun is too much" for BE "The weather is very sunny"; "The wind is too much" for BE "The weather is very windy"; "The rain is too much" for BE "The weather is very wet"; "The cold is too much" for BE "The weather is very cold."

top-notcher   formed from "top-notch". BE has the adjective "top-notch" which means "excellent", "of the highest quality", as in "a top-notch lawyer". But there is no such noun as "top-notcher" in BE. In NE, this noun means "highly placed people", as in "The wedding was witnessed by many top-notchers in government and the business community."

---

torch-light many NE speakers use "torch-light" in free variation with BE "torch", i.e. an electric lamp functioning by means of a battery. BE usage prefers to use "torch" as a simplified form of the compound "torch-light."

tout in NE, a tout refers to someone (usually of indecent character) who stays around motor parks with the aim of helping to load vehicles on commission. In BE, the verb "tout" denotes "to try to get people to buy one's goods or services, especially by approaching them directly." The use of "tout" in NE is pejorative.

towel used as a NE slang to refer to the lining of the stomach of cows, which is often eaten as meat. In the meat section of every Nigerian market, it is common to hear such utterances as "Do you have towel?"; "Customer, give me some towel."

traditional marriage in Nigeria, there are several kinds of marriages: church marriage/wedding (for Christians), Islamic marriage or fatia, court marriage/registry, and traditional marriage, also known as "engagement ceremony" (particularly among the Yoruba). Also known as "Igba nkwu nwaanyi" among the Igbo, traditional marriage is the aspect of marriage in which the man taking a wife has to fulfill the traditional marriage rites. In most cases, traditional marriage takes place before registry and church wedding. It is common to read invitation cards which state: "The families of Chief and Mrs. T. I. Igwe of Ezeoke, Nsu and Dr. and Mrs. Ibezim of Ihiteowerri, Orlu cordially invite Chief/

Dr./Mr./Mrs. ... to the Igba nkwu nwaanyi / traditional marriage of their daughter Miss ... and their son Mr. ..."

traditional wrestling wrestling that is seen to be part of the culture of some tribes in Nigeria which is aimed at entertainment while identifying very strong persons. The winner is one who is able to throw down the other in a way that his back touches the ground.

transport money in NE, "transport money" is equivalent to BE "money for transport" or "money for fare", e.g. "He could not come as planned because he did not have transport money."

travel in NE, "travel" is often used with the meaning "go on a journey" so that it is common to hear such utterances as "He has traveled", "She traveled". It is normal in BE to state the destination of the journey, thus "He has traveled to London", "She traveled to Osogbo."

tribalism often used to mean favouritism towards one from one's tribe or discrimination against one from another ethnic or tribal group, e.g. "Nigerian politicians are always promoting tribalism for their selfish goals." "Tribalism" in BE refers to "the organization of a social group into a tribe."

tribal marks face marks usually given at birth associated with some ethnic groups in Nigeria, e.g. "He described him as a fat man with a very large belly and curious tribal marks cut on his face."

trickish used in NE where BE uses "tricky" meaning "crafty" or "deceitful", e.g. "She is very trickish" for BE

"She is very tricky." The use of "trickish" has become obsolete in BE usage, but is very commonly used in NE.

trouble often collocates with "meet/see" with the meaning "to land oneself in difficulties"; "to find oneself in trouble", e.g. "You are now behaving as if you are above the law, when you meet trouble, no one is going to assist you"; "When my husband comes back, you will see trouble."

trouble-shooter used to mean "trouble-maker", as in "Riot policemen in the area have intensified their patrol warning trouble-shooters to stay away or face their wrath." In BE, "trouble-shooter" is a person who makes peace. (Also in WAE).

trouser trouser is often used as an ellipsis for "a pair of trousers" or "trousers", e.g. "He bought two trousers for me" instead of "He bought two pairs of trousers for me."

try frequently used in NE with the meaning "make a considerable achievement", as in "He has tried"; "You tried." These two expressions could be used in contexts where BE would use "Well done."

Try-your-luck lottery usually a tick card of A-4 paper with pictures of different items on it and with the winning item sealed by the middle of the card. It is opened at the end of the competition of the lottery game and the winner is given some food items and provisions.

tufia! /tufia/ spitting action; an interjection that expresses disgust. (SL: Igbo).

turn one's head idiomatic expression often found in NE in the register of love, meaning "make to fall deeply in love", as in "She has turned the man's head." This NE idiomatic expression may be loosely equivalent to BE "turn somebody on", i.e. "to excite or stimulate somebody, especially sexually", as in "She gets turned on by men in uniform."

turn the soup stir the soup, as in "Ijeoma is turning the soup" for BE "Ijeoma is stirring the soup inside the pot."

tutor in NE, this noun primarily denotes a secondary school teacher. In BE, "tutor" denotes a university teacher who supervises the studies of a student.

tuwo /tuwo/ food prepared from rice or guinea-corn. (SL: Hausa).

Twelve-two-third the mathematical maneuvering that characterized the resolution of the presidential election stalemate of 1979 which saw the National Party of Nigeria (NPN) to power." NPN was said to have won elections in twelve-two-third states in Nigeria.

two many speakers of NE use "two" where BE uses "both", e.g. "He met two of them" for BE "He met both of them."

U

ubangiji /ʊbangidʒi/ the supreme deity. (SL: Hausa).

ube /ube/ pear tree; the edible pear fruit of Dacroydes edules, eaten after softening in hot ash or water, e.g. "Most people in this part of the country like eating maize with ube." (SL: Igbo).

UBE an abbreviation for Universal Basic Education—a body set up to harmonise Federal government's educational policies, especially at the lower educational levels.

ubo /ʊbɔ/ musical instrument made from thin bamboo slivers on base of calabash half, or of 'okwe' wood, like flat bars, and strings of variable length; guitar; xylophone, as in "Playing ubo is my hobby." (SL: Igbo).

udara /ʊdara/ a kind of apple; yellowish ball-like fruit (of Chrysophylum africanum), of tomato-like flesh, usually with five or six hard seeds, and tastes bitter sweet.

Udoji Commission /udodʒi kɔmiʃɔn/ a popular commission that undertook job evaluation exercise in the entire public service in 1974 and awarded salary increase to public servants.

udu /udu/ musical instrument made from clay pot with

narrow neck, wide brim, and extra hole at the side; sometimes called the 'resonating pot', e.g. "During festive periods, women entertain the public by playing udu and blowing whistles." (SL: Igbo).

ugba /ʊgba/ oil bean seed; oil bean tree; dish of finely sliced and slightly fermented oil-bean prepared with spices, fish, or meat; also known as local salad, it is a delicacy prepared from the seeds of Pentaclethra macrophylla, popular among the Igbo. (SL: Igbo).

ugu /ʊgʊ/ pumpkin; plant (of Telfaria occidentalis) whose seeds and leaves are used in food preparation. While its leaves serve in the preparation of soup, as in "Ugu soup", its seeds are cooked and eaten. (SL: Igbo).

uha /ʊha/ a particular vegetable used in making soup, popular among the Igbo, as in "Ugha soup". See also ora. (SL: Igbo).

ukazi /ʊkazi/ green-coloured vegetable (hard in nature) and used for making soup and also for the preparation of "African salad." It is popular among people from the Eastern Nigeria. (SL: Efik).

ukpa /ʊkpa/ kind of slightly bitter edible fruit with thin hard skin. (SL: Igbo).

Ulama a Muslim cleric, as in "The Clergy and the Ulama, the traditional rulers and other opinion leaders have a vital role to play in educating their flock, subjects and audiences on the dangers of prostitution and women trafficking." (SL: Arabic).

---

umuada /ʊmʊada/ direct female descendants; daughters of the kindred; women born to the kindred, excluding women married into the kindred; a group of women who are related in Igbo traditional society. Many of them may be married outside their domain, but each time they come back to their village for a ceremony such as burial, they wield so much power, e.g. "Then the umuada, direct female descendants of Ojemba, sent word that they would come and open the house." (SL: Igbo).

umunna /ʊmʊnna/ kinsmen; sons of the kindred; men born to the kindred; direct male descendants; a group of men who are related, e.g. "A few days after Chiaku had arrived, Oji invited all the umunna to his house." Umunna is a system of patrilineal organization, which determines one's membership of a patrilineage as well as rights, obligations and benefits accruing from such membership. (SL: Igbo).

uncle also used as a mode of address to any male adult, usually by younger persons, even if only an acquaintance of the parents. It is also sometimes used as an address of respect to strangers, especially in contexts where favour is sought, or in the market where a trader wants to attract a buyer, as in "Uncle, what do you want to buy?" In BE, the term is normally limited to the parents' brothers and close male friends. See also the use of auntie. (Also in WAE).

under based on analogy with "under repair", "under arrest", etc., the preposition "under" is often used, especially among the less educated NE speakers to collocate with some words in contexts different from BE usage, e.g. "She is under pregnancy" for BE "She is pregnant"; "You have to give me my money today under must" for BE "You have to give me my money today, obligatorily." The second example occurs in NE only in colloquial contexts.

under the sun "under" replaces "in" in the NE expression "stand under the sun" which is equivalent to BE "stand in the sun", e.g. "Don't stand under the sun" for BE "Don't stand in the sun."

understand some NE speakers use this word in the continuous form, e.g. "Are you understanding me?" This verb is rarely found in the continuous form in BE.

underwear this word is often found in the plural form in NE and used only for "underpants", e.g. "I bought a new set of underwears and singlets yesterday." In BE, "underwear" is normally treated as a non-count noun and so is not found in the plural form. Its meaning includes both underpants and upper underwear.

unfortunate legs used idiomatically to apologise to one who has just come at a time the host is finishing his food. This context is lacking in English culture, e.g. "You have unfortunate legs."

unless "unless" is a conjunction in BE, but it is often used in NE in the context of buying and selling as a preposition in an elliptical statement to mean "except" or "only", e.g.:

A: Do you have coke?
B: Unless fanta.
The BE equivalent of NE response might be "No, except Fanta" or "No, only Fanta."

up NE speakers often insert this word after verbs in contexts where it would be considered unnecessary in BE. Such verbs include: come (as in "Has it come up to that?"); cope (as in "He could no longer cope up with the two jobs"); cover ("Our mathematics teacher could not cover up the syllabus"); end (as in "Let me end up this speech by thanking all of you for your sacrifice"); fill (as in "The management directed that more workers be employed to fill up the vacant positions"); finish (as in "Finish up the food"); keep (as in "She always keeps up her promise"); pay (as in "I have paid up all my debt"), raise (as in "Raise up your hands"); and rise (as in "The child rises up very early.")

up and down it commonly denotes an attire where the top and the trousers or the shorts or the wrapper are of the same material and colour. For women, it denotes a two-piece wrapper (down), with one tied over the other. The upper piece (up) is a blouse made of the same material and worn over the lower piece, which reaches to the ankle. The lower piece may also be a skirt or a pair of trousers. For men, it refers to a two-piece suit or any other piece of clothing with the upper and lower piece made of the same material. For school children, it denotes a uniformed wear where the shirt and the shorts/trousers are of the same material and colour, e.g.

"Is this material enough for up and down?"

upliftment based on analogy with "resentment", for instance, "upliftment" is commonly used in NE but not in BE, e.g. "The new regime has demonstrated that it is committed towards the upliftment of the standard of living of all Nigerians." The equivalent form of this word in BE is "uplifting"—increase in standing and respect, but perhaps, "improvement" would be more likely in the above sentence. (Also in WAE).

UPN an abbreviation for Unity Party of Nigeria, one of Nigeria's political parties during the second republic.

upon "upon" is a preposition in BE, but is often treated as a conjunction in NE to mean "in spite of ", e.g. "Upon all the money I gave him for his marriage, he still went and collected some loan."

upper commonly used, especially among the less educated speakers of NE, to collocate with names of days of the week, week or month, in an adverbial expression referring to future time, e.g. "I won't be around next week. Check me the upper week." "Check me the upper week" will be equivalent to BE "Check me the week after next." There are also "upper Monday", "upper Tuesday", "upper month", etc.

upstair often used especially at the lower educational level to describe a building with several floors, as in "My father has an upstair in the village." "One upstair" in NE would mean "a two storey building."

uselessed wasted, as in "She uselessed my money" for

BE "She wasted my money" or "She extravagantly spent my money."

utazi /ʊtazi/ a particular vegetable, usually bitter, and used in making soup, pepper soup, etc. popular among people from eastern Nigeria. (SL: **Igbo**).

V

vendor in NE, "vendor" denotes a person, usually a teenager or sometimes an older person who sells newspapers and magazines either by hawking them around or by staying in a place. Interested buyers usually attract his attention by calling or shouting "Vendor!" In BE, "news vendor" may be used to refer to one who sells newspapers but he usually stays at a place. Similarly, newspapers are commonly available in Britain for purchase in bookshops, shops and supermarkets, which usually reserve a section of its space for the sale of newspapers and magazines.

very some speakers of NE insert "very" between two parts of a reflexive pronoun for emphasis, as in "my very self", e.g.:
A: I saw you removing the book from the table.
B: My very self?
"My very self" in this context is equivalent to the emphatic pronoun in BE "I myself."

very essential the adverb "very" substitutes for "most" in the NE collocation "very essential" which is equivalent to BE "most essential", as in "It is very essential at this stage of the transition programme that we have a principled and honest man like you in government."

---

video ellipsis for "video recorder", "video player" or "video cassette", so that when a Nigerian says "I want to buy a video", he may be referring to any of these. (Also in WAE).

view some speakers of NE, especially those belonging to lower educational level, use the base form of a verb after the phrase "with a view to", e.g. "I am studying chemistry, physics and mathematics with a view to read medicine". In BE, the gerund is preferred, as in "I am studying chemistry, physics and mathematics with a view to reading medicine."

village in Nigeria, "village refers to a rural area in contrast to the city or town. In Nigeria but not in Britain, everybody is associated with an ancestral home, which in most cases is a rural area. The term "village" is therefore used to refer to this rural location, e.g. "She objected to the idea of having his daughter brought up in the village by his mother in-law."

VIP an abbreviation for Very Important Person, as in "Everybody should help in keeping the village clean because we are expecting many VIPs during the New Yam Festival."

Vision 2010 a masterplan to turn Nigeria into an industrial nation in the first decade of the twenty-first century, e.g. "In a society that is ruled by honest and honourable men, you ought to be invited by members of the so-called Vision 2010 for further discussions on how best to launch Nigeria into the information age."

---

voire out in NE, the particle "out" often follows the verb "voice", i.e. "to express one's feelings verbally", in contexts where it will not be found in BE, e.g. "The labour leader voiced out the workers' grievances." In BE usage, the particle "out" will be considered redundant in this sentence.

voluminous some NE users, especially students often describe a book as being voluminous where BE would accept "very long", as in "He admitted that he was discouraged from reading physics because of the voluminous nature of their texts."

voluntary donation often used tautologically in NE but not in BE, as in "What is interpreted today as levy was initially intended as voluntary donation." BE speakers would not use 'voluntary' and 'donation' together because 'donation' also implies gift or giving voluntarily.

W

wahala /wahala/ "trouble", as in "Super Eagles brought style into relaxation after triumph when they forgot football and all its wahala momentarily, to enjoy a game of 'head-tennis', Saturday."

wait for one's turn the preposition "for" is often inserted in NE expression "Wait for one's turn" which is equivalent to BE "Wait one's turn", i.e. waiting his chance to strike. E.g. "Wait for your turn" for BE "Wait your turn."

walahi! /walai/ an interjection commonly used in northern Nigeria, especially among Muslims, it is an emphatic expression of truth, which may be equivalent to "by God", as in:
A: I can assure you, you need skill and experience to win them and that is why I am organizing this kind of friendly games for you, or are you angry?
B: Walahi! I am not angry sir. (SL: Hausa).

walking stick stick, which is designed to aid walking, and used especially by old people, the sick, and sometimes as a fashion that goes with traditional outfit, e.g. "The chief, who appeared in all white attire and with a walking stick, called for peace through out the celebration period."

want many NE speakers use "want to" in a wide range of contexts with inanimate subjects to mean "about to", as in "Kerosene wants to finish in the stove." This will be equivalent in BE to "Kerosene is about to finish in the stove"; "It wants to rain" for BE "It looks as if it's going to rain." (Also in WAE).

wash used as a NE slang to mean "celebrate". It is commonly used in the context of making some achievements such as the purchase of a new or used car, promotion in a job or appointment to a higher position, admission to a higher educational institution, etc. The celebration that is referred to as "washing" is usually in the form of eating and/or drinking, along with prayers, praises and sometimes dancing. "Wash" is also used in NE with the meaning "insult" or "abuse", as in "I thoroughly washed him for telling lies."

wash eyes "wash your eyes in water" is idiomatically used with the meaning "to be careful", e.g. "What I have come to tell you is that you must wash your eyes in water." This context is lacking in the British culture.

wash films "develop" or "print" films, e.g. "He has gone to the photo studio to wash some films." In BE, "wash" does not collocate with films in the same context as above.

wash mouth "to brush the teeth", as in "Let me wash my mouth" for BE "Let me brush my teeth."

watchnight a term for "night watchman."

water bottle bottle containing water, equivalent to BE

"bottle for water". But "water bottle" is always associated with children. It is used to put their water and other liquid food. Usually with soft narrow mouth, it is sometimes called "feeding bottle", especially when it serves for water and for food. Sometimes, "water bottle" is used to mean "bottle for water" usually put in the fridge, so that when one asks "Where is our water bottle?" one is very likely referring to this sense.

water leaf the green vegetable of Talinum triangulare; usually found as a weed, but can also be cultivated and consumed as vegetable. In the preparation of what is known as 'vegetable soup', it is often mixed with other vegetables.

waterproof also used as a noun to mean "cellophane" (bag or paper). As a noun, "waterproof" in BE denotes a waterproof garment.

water-yam the tuber of Dioscorea alata Lin; large tubers with dark-brown skin and white or pink flesh often the size of normal yams.

wayo /wajo/ "cheating", "dishonesty", "deceit", e.g. "A presidential aspirant has accused NECON of wayo for embarking on an endless amendment to the electoral guidelines and the transitional programme." (SL: Pidgin).

wayo man a confident trickster, as in "You are a wayo man." (SL: Pidgin).

wayward in BE, "wayward" is an adjective meaning "not easily controlled; rather wild: a wayward child."

In NE, when one is said to be wayward, it is simply interpreted that the person (often a woman) is a prostitute or a flirt.

weave-on artificial hair worn by women. It is woven onto the natural hair for more elegant looks.

wee wee /wi:wi:/ colloquially used for Indian hemp or marijuana. (SL: Pidgin).

weekend the sense of weekend in Nigeria differs slightly from the sense in which it is used in BE. In Nigeria, weekend starts from Friday (after working period) to Sunday, but in Britain, it is Saturday and Sunday.

welcome 1. greeting for one who has just arrived from a journey or from any outing.
2. often used with a past tense suffix in NE in contexts where it functions in BE as an adjective, e.g. "Your advice is extremely welcomed" for BE "Your advice is extremely welcome."

welcome address NE speakers prefer this condensed noun phrase without a preposition to its BE version "an address of welcome", e.g. "The University Vice Chancellor delivered a welcome address which was immediately followed by donations" for BE "The University Vice Chancellor delivered an address of welcome, which was immediately followed by donations."

well done greeting to someone at work, or even to someone relaxing. "Well done sir" may just be a polite way of thanking an older man who has invited one to come and share his food, an invitation which may have been turned down. In BE, "Well done" is used to praise someone for the work or feat he has already achieved.

well-well colloquially used for "sufficiently", "very much", e.g. "Customer, put jara well-well." This sentence is a request by a buyer to the seller to make enough discount in the form of addition to the quantity of what is being bought.

wet when used in collocation with flowers, "wet" is used in the sense of BE "water", as in "He has gone to wet the flowers" for BE "He has gone to water the flowers."

wetin you carry derogatorily used to refer to the Nigeria police, and derived from the frequent police attitude of stopping passenger buses or taxis with the question "Wetin you carry?" meaning "What are you carrying in your vehicle?"—a search often meant to extort money from transporters and commuters alike, e.g. "The President, Chief Olusegun Obasanjo has asked the Nigeria Police to stop wetin-you-carry attitude."

what is good for the goose "good" replaces "sauce" in NE expression "What is good for the goose is good for the gander" which is equivalent to BE "What is sauce for the goose is sauce for the gander", i.e. if one person is allowed to behave in a certain way, then so is the other person.

what of frequently used in the context of buying and

selling to haggle about price, e.g.:
Seller: The price is ten Naira.
Buyer: What of five Naira?
Since the buying and selling conventions are different
in Britain, this usage is lacking in BE.

what of if often found in NE for BE "What if", e.g.
"What of if I die tomorrow?" for BE "What if I die
tomorrow?"

what's-up used as a noun in NE with the meaning
"irresponsible", e.g. "She is a what's up" for "She is
irresponsible." "What's-up?" is an American English
expression which came into NE and was popularized
by a group of young people whose behaviour was seen
to be "irresponsible".

where? "where?" is often heard in NE as an ellipsis for
the question "Where are you going to?" or "Where are
you coming from?" Similarly, the question "For where?"
is jocularly asked rather rhetorically as a way of
debunking a friendly accusation or teasing, as in:
A: I was told you have bought a new car.
B. For where?

whisk "whisk away", meaning to "take somebody away
quickly and suddenly" is associated with informal style
in BE, but it is widely used in NE in both formal and
informal styles, e.g. "The opposition leader was whisked
away by the police in the early hours of yesterday." (Also
in WAE).

whiteman formed in agglutination for BE 'white man'.

---

white pepper   made from the mature berry of Piper plant; usually milder than the black pepper and also used as seasoning.

white-yam   white textured yam which usually tastes good. The name "white yam" distinguishes this variety from other varieties of yam produced all over the country.

who and who   a reduplicative used in both formal and informal styles to denote number, as in "You should please tell us who and who you have so far invited for the party." BE does not duplicate "who" in this manner to denote plural, and therefore, "who and who" in this example would be "who has" or simply "the persons."

whole   BE uses "whole" to stress fullness or completeness, as in "The whole town was destroyed by flood." But NE speakers sometimes put "whole" before pronouns or proper names, to express the disappointment that someone is associated with something very belittling, e.g. "a whole you" (as big as you are), "a whole John" (as big as John is).

wife   "wife" is used in BE to denote a married woman, especially when considered in relation to her husband. In NE usage, the person addressed as "our wife" may just be a relative's wife. This sense is absent in the BE context.

wildwest   street riots and bloodshed throughout western Nigeria caused by massive rigging in 1965 elections. Ever since, the southwestern Nigeria is often referred to as the wildwest in the context of violent political behaviour, e.g. "We·have tried to turn the wildwest into a wise west but to no avail."

win some speakers of NE use "win" to also mean "defeat" or "beat", e.g. "In a professional league division one match played last weekend in Enugu, Rangers won Shooting Stars by two goals to nothing" BE uses "win" in the sense of obtaining or achieving something, as in "He won first prize."

wipe the particle "out" often follows the verb "wipe" in contexts where it will not occur in BE, e.g. "I wiped out the tears from her eyes." In BE usage, this particle will be considered redundant.

wise often used in NE where BE would use "clever", "intelligence", or "sensible", as in:
A: My little son realised that the dog was about to bite him and he quickly stopped playing with it.
B: He is too wise for his age.
"Wise" is used in BE in the context of having or showing good judgement based on knowledge and experience, as in "a wise man."

with immediate effect a phrase, which is frequently associated with military regimes, suggesting immediacy of action, as in "My government has directed the contractors handling this road to commence work on the road with immediate effect"; "All the political parties in Nigeria have been banned with immediate effect."

---

with the hope in the hope, as in "We went there with the hope of resolving the dispute" for BE "We went there in the hope of resolving the dispute."

woman wrapper used idiomatically as a derogatory way of referring to a man who is easily exploited by women, e.g. "John is a woman wrapper. He hardly can say no to his wife.".

wonderful also used as an exclamation to express grief, alarm, disgust, surprise or even admiration. It may be equivalent in BE to "What a pity!", "Incredible!", "Fantastic!", etc., e.g.:
A: The result of the lottery is now out and I won the first prize.
B: Wonderful!
In BE, "wonderful" is used as an adjective to describe something pleasant or enjoyable, as in "a wonderful occasion" or "a wonderful person."

wood the plural form of this noun is often found in NE but not in BE where it is used as a mass noun, e.g. "He has removed all the woods" for BE "He has removed all the wood."

working-class often used by some NE speakers in contexts where BE would prefer "working population", i.e. those whose age constitutes the working group. In this sense, children, students, retired as well as very old people, are excluded from the working population. To many Nigerians, "working-class" denotes all those with regularly paid jobs, as in "It has always been his ambition to marry a working-class woman." In BE, however, "working-class" is used in contrast to the "middle class", and strictly defined on the basis of income, occupation and status. Those who essentially belong to the working-class in Britain are manual workers.

working-place commonly used, especially by the less educated NE speakers to denote "office", as in "Check him in his working-place" for BE "Check him in his office."

workmanship commonly used, especially at the lower educational level to denote "labour", e.g. "If you want this job done today, you have to bring some money for the materials and also for workmanship immediately." In BE, "workmanship" denotes a person's skill in working, as in "He was praised for his workmanship."

would there is a general tendency for NE speakers to use "would" in contexts where BE would prefer "will" probably because "would" is perceived to be more polite than "will". Examples are: "The party would begin at 12 noon"; "It is our hope that the coming year would be better than this year." In both examples, BE would probably use "will". BE usage prefers the "will" form when the message to be communicated is not doubtful or uncertain. However, BE speakers use "would" in several circumstances among which is for describing the consequence of an imagined event, e.g. "She would be finer with make-up"; "It would be unfortunate if we miss the flight."

wrapper "waist wrap" or "waist cloth", frequently used

---

by women and sometimes by men, especially for sleeping or for relaxation, as in "Soon Christie was wiping tears of joy with the corners of her wrapper."

write some speakers of NE sometimes redundantly use "in black and white" and "write" in the same sentence, e.g. "The only way by which your request can be considered is for you to write it down in black and white." BE speakers will consider "black and white" redundant in this sentence.

wuruwuru /wuruwuru/ dishonesty; cheating, as in "There is much of wuruwuru in the market today" for BE "There is much cheating in the market today." (SL: Pidgin).

Y

yab /jab/ a. slang popularly used in Nigerian Pidgin and sometimes in NE meaning "remark freely and insultingly about someone or event." "Yabbis" is a noun derived from "yab", as in "The musicians have promised a lot of entertaining shows including yabbis."

yam a very popular tuber similar to potato used as one of Nigeria's staple food. It may be cooked, pounded or fried for eating. There are many varieties of yam, of different sizes and shapes.

yandaba /jandaba/ a group of social miscreants or street urchins popularly found in Kano and other big cities in the northern part of Nigeria, e.g. "Government's promise of security could not save the Yoruba as the notorious Yandaba came calling again." In the south, these miscreants are known as "area boys."

yauwa /jowa/ an interjection which expresses strong agreement or approval. (SL: Hausa).

yellow a NE way of describing a fellow Black who is fairly light-skinned, as in "We are all yellow in my family" for BE "We are all light-skinned in my family." It is also used as a form of address to those who are light-skinned as in when a street beggar says "Yellow, give me some money." However, since "yellow" is seen to be the ultimate complexion, a beggar may call one yellow not necessarily because he/she is light-skinned but as a flattery to attract some alms.

yellow-carded sometimes used to mean to receive yellow card in a football march, e.g. "The team captain was yellow-carded." See also "red-carded."

yellow fever commonly used as a slang for a special cadre of traffic policemen, obviously because of the interpretation of their orange-coloured shirts as yellow. BE usage is familiar only with its medical denotation, i.e. an infectious tropical disease that causes the skin to turn yellow.

yesterday night often heard where BE would prefer "last night", e.g. "I saw her yesterday night" for BE "I saw her last night."

yeye /jeje/ never-do-well; "useless", as in "Yeye man" meaning "Useless man". The sentence, "All that sorrow was yeye" would be equivalent to BE "All that sorrow was useless." (SL: Pidgin).

Yoruba /joruba/ stands for the name and the language of one of the three major ethnic groups in Nigeria.

you meet us well a polite way of inviting a visitor who has just arrived when food is being eaten to come and join in eating the meal.

you people often used as an emphatic plural form of "you" or "you all", as in "You people are not always around." In BE, "you" is a pronoun that may have singular or plural reference depending on the context.

your people "How are your people?" is an inquiry frequently heard in exchange of greetings among Nigerians. "Your people" here may be referring to relations or members of the extended family. This context is lacking in the English culture.

Z

Zango /zango/ large centralised Hausa community found in most cities in West Africa. The term originally referred to the 'stopping point of trade caravans.' In cities outside primarily Islamic areas, the Zango will usually be the centre of organized Islamic activities, such as Koranic schools and sites for the major Islamic festivals. (SL: Hausa).

zero allocation frequently heard in the context of revenue allocation, particularly among Local Government Areas. The Federal Government deducts, from source, monies paid on behalf of Local Governments (especially in respect of payment of primary school teachers' salaries) and hands over to them their balance, which is described as zero allocation because of its perceived insuffiency, e.g. "Governor Lam Adesina of Oyo State has asked the Federal Government to urgently resolve the issue of zero allocations to Local Governments to enable them to pay their workers' salary."

zinc /ziŋk/ commonly used with the meaning "corrugated metal roof", as in "He is about to roof his house but he still has two more bundles of zinc to buy."

zombie   /zombi/ a NE slang for referring to Nigerian soldiers. This was invented and popularised in the 1970s by a well-known controversial Nigerian musician. The dictionary defines zombie as "a dull slow person who seems to act without thinking or not to be aware of what is happening around her or him."

Printed in the United States
216579BV00004B/1/A